# YOUR CHILD'S TODDLER YEARS

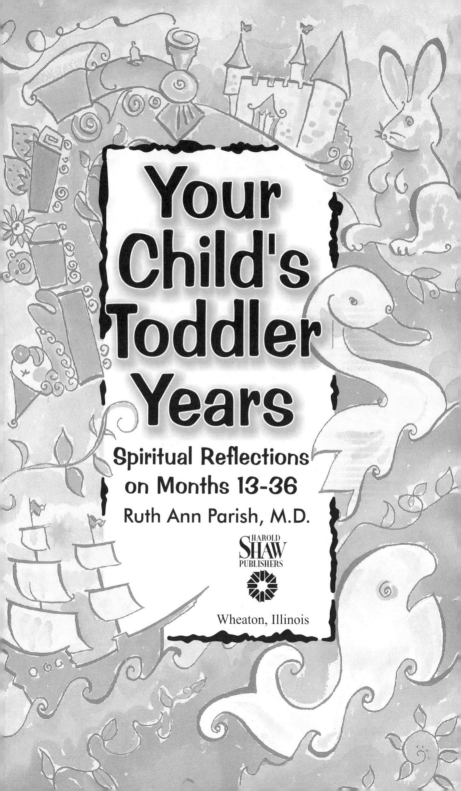

# Your Child's Toddler Years

## Spiritual Reflections on Months 13-36

### Ruth Ann Parish, M.D.

HAROLD
SHAW
PUBLISHERS

Wheaton, Illinois

ISBN 0-87788-924-4

Photos courtesy of Craig and Cheryl Donaldson, Graeme and Ann Findlay, Jim and Rosanna Lin, Shawn and Shari Maxwell, Paul and Michelle Wescombe

Cover and interior art by David LaPlaca
Cover and interior design by Thomas Leo

**Library of Congress Cataloging-in-Publication Data**

Parish, Ruth Ann, 1951-
    Your child's toddler years : spiritual reflections on months 13-36 / by Ruth Ann Parish.
       p.  cm.
    Includes bibliographical references.
    ISBN 0-87788-924-4 (pbk.)
    1. Parents—Religious life.  2. Parenting—Religious aspects—Christianity.
3. Child development.   I. Title
BV4845.P38  1999
155.42'2—dc21                                                                99-3517
                                               CIP

04   03   02   01   00   99

10  9  8  7  6  5  4  3  2  1

*To my grandmother, Ruth Ann Parish (Sr.!),*
*who taught me the value of humor*

# Contents

# Acknowledgments

I am grateful to the following folks for help with this effort: to Elisa Fryling, who edited this volume with grace and clarity; to Joan Guest and the folks at Harold Shaw Publishers, who believed in taking a chance on "something different"; to the friends and family who supported me through this project; to KT and Ben, my own personal reminders of God's amazing grace and love; to BJ, who helps keep my creative self alive; and to God the Creator, Redeemer, and Sustainer, whose love makes all things possible.

# Introduction:
## "T" Is for Toddler

Welcome to the world of toddlers! By now you have been privileged to watch your infant, so small and helpless, become a much more self-sufficient child.

You may have taken time to reflect on the miracles of the past year: your infant has learned to hold her* head up, move her eyes together, grasp objects with one or both hands, sit by herself, crawl, pull to a stand, cruise the furniture, pull objects off the coffee table, completely rearrange the folded laundry in the basket, communicate using body language and possibly some words, recognize loved ones and differentiate them from strangers, feed herself and chew the food using real teeth, and perhaps she has even learned to walk. All of these tricks, and more, she has mastered in twelve months. It's been quite a year for both you and your toddler.

---

* Gender pronoun references will alternate by chapter.

Now you are making the transition from being the parent of an infant to being the parent of a toddler, and it is a *big* transition. This past year, your child's development centered around motor skills and cognitive skills. In the coming two years, your child will develop further cognitive and social/language skills, but also large motor skills. Your child will be harder to keep track of, harder to convince not to climb on something and jump off of it, harder to reason with in many ways.

You may sometimes feel that aliens have arrived in the middle of the night, taken away your sweet, innocent child, and left an "evil twin" in her place. All of these feelings are normal for the parents of toddlers. In fact, if you *don't* want to trade your toddler in for a new model, or perhaps for a used car (or even a toaster) at some point in the next two years, you run the risk of being thought abnormal by friends and family. Let's face it: toddlers can be hard to live with. In fact, they can border on being *impossible* to live with. But then, so can adults.

> **Toddlers can be hard to live with. But then, so can adults.**

## Grace under Fire

Making it through your child's second and third years of life involves a lot of positive self-talk, survival strategies, and a good measure of grace. There will be times when you inwardly (or outwardly) scream in frustration; so will your toddler. There will be times when you *know* that your way is the better choice; your toddler will think the same thing about her way. There will be moments when you think "if I could only use language to reason with her, I know she'd see it my way"; so will your child.

Surviving the toddler years is one of the marks of true parenthood. It's a real-life "combat zone," and one that often requires a mindset similar to those brave souls who participate in outdoor survival programs: you have to begin by believing that you *will* survive. You must believe you are capable of doing what is needed to maneuver both you and your toddler to the far side of three years old. Then, you have to develop the strategy of living *in the moment,* which often means that you have to focus on today, not worry about tomorrow, or next month, or Christmas with the relatives. Just get this next toehold, grab the next limb of the tree, take that next step, and the journey will take care of itself. That, my friend, is faith in action.

Another strategy that is essential to parenting a toddler: don't take anything too personally. If at all possible, avoid putting your entire self-esteem and skill as a parent on the line with every negative encounter. Just because limits have to be set and you are the one to set those limits doesn't mean that you are a "bad" parent. In fact, it means that you are a very *good* parent. Physical limits must be set—no one allows a toddler to run into the street by herself. Your toddler isn't *trying* to be negative, or "impossible," or too active. She's just doing the developmentally appropriate thing for her age—she is in process! Isn't it nice to know that God encourages each of us "in process" and doesn't condemn us for our faltering attempts?

So, I will say it again: even though toddlerhood has its challenges for both the toddler and the parent, you *will* arrive at the other side of the process with a bright, enthusiastic, articulate, and curious three year old on your hands and in your heart.

### Enjoying the adventure

Parenting a toddler is a supreme lesson in the meaning of the word *patience*. What a wonderful opportunity you've been given to explore this aspect of the fruit of the Spirit (see Galatians 5:22). Perhaps you didn't think you'd ever make it through labor and delivery; but you did. Maybe you worried that you'd never know how to care for an infant; but you learned. And just possibly, right now, you're looking at your ever-more-mobile one year old and thinking to yourself, "I'll never get through this phase."

> **Parenting a toddler is a supreme lesson in the meaning of the word *patience*.**

But, you *will* get to the top of the mountain. You will get to the place of seeing the beautiful vista, with the help of the Creator of this toddler. And the more you can remember that you are *not* in this all alone, the easier it will become to live through each day.

I believe that the toddler years are one of the real

stretching points of parenting. But God never gives us more than we can bear. When you've lived with a toddler, you have seen the mountains *and* the valleys, and you develop a new confidence and (we hope) calm attitude towards the parenting process for the years to come. So here's to the adventure before you!

### The organization of this book

I know that parents of toddlers are in need of *time* as well as patience, so in this book I've divided the chapters into a series of short reflections on your child's physiological development and what that development can teach all of us about God and about ourselves. I have arranged large motor, small motor, and language skills into "age windows" because when children reach toddlerhood, they begin to vary more in their developmental progress from child to child. For instance, some children walk at ten months, some walk at fourteen months. Some children talk well at fifteen months, some don't talk well until thirty months. There is greater individual variation between toddlers than between infants for several reasons.

First, body type will, to some extent, determine the timing and accuracy of large motor skills. Those toddlers who are "scrawny," well-muscled, and thin will naturally tend to explore the large motor skills with more enthusiasm, and probably with more skill, than the child who is in the ninety-fifth percentile in weight and the fortieth percentile in height.

Second, environment plays a role. A child who spends several hours each week in a daycare setting, with slightly older children around her, will push herself to perform some of the motor skills earlier than will the child who is home alone with an adult all day. The daycare child may or may not attempt language skills earlier than the home-based child. Certainly the child who is being raised in a multilingual environment may be slower to attain words in English than the child who hears only English in the home. This is a temporary slowness and is far outweighed by the innate advantages of a multilingual background by the age of five years.

Third, learning styles vary among children. The kinesthetic learner, the one who learns by (and while) moving, will emphasize the large motor skills in the early months of toddlerhood. Conversely, the highly visual child may be content to sit and *look* around the room, thinking about objects and relationships without needing to touch them. The auditory learner will seek new experiences through sounds and language, and may be an early talker but not walk until fourteen months.

In general, I find that toddlers fall loosely into one of two camps: either they are large motor skills kids early on, or they are small motor-language skills kids early on. Whichever type your toddler is, be assured that she will gain all of the skills. It will take some time, and she may not look stunning next to the twelve-month-old child with a five-hundred-word vocabulary, but all children arrive at age three with approximately the same sets of skills in all groups.

As a mother of two and a pediatrician, I know firsthand how much we can learn about God from children. Remaining alert to what God has to say to you about your toddler may make you more able to help that child explore her own spiritual journey someday. In these first years of life—in the midst of tantrums and tumbles and giggles and growth—be aware of the rich opportunity to learn the truth of Jesus' words about children, for "the kingdom of heaven belongs to such as these" (Matthew 19:14).

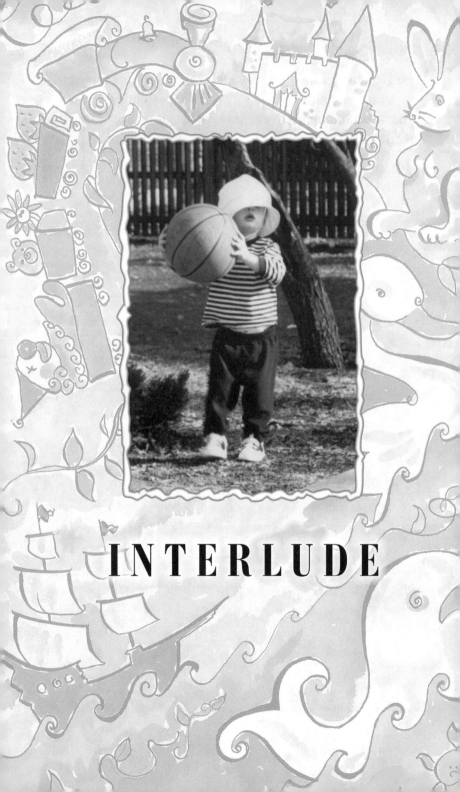

# INTERLUDE

# Parish's Maxims for the Toddler Years

Over the years as a pediatrician and a parent, I've developed a set of practical helps for moms and dads. Following are a few things that parents have the right to keep in mind during their child's toddlerhood. These are:

*1. Parents do better with sleep.* Isn't this as true in the toddler years as it was during infancy? Isn't it, in fact, one of the basic tenets of parenting? You will find that your toddler may challenge this universal constant once or twice between the ages of one and three. So it is still a useful law to keep in mind, and one that I remind all my little toddler patients to consider before they call out for Mommy or Daddy at two in the morning. Even though Scripture reminds us that our parent God never slumbers or sleeps, human parents need to occasionally.

*2. Parents and pediatricians never get any older, of course.* This maxim is particularly useful for the parents of an eighteen to twenty-four month old to reflect on. These are the people who chase an active toddler around the house all day, keeping her from climbing the curtains and eating the dog food out of the dog's dish. They chase toddlers down the corridors of shopping malls and down the hallways at the doctor's office, knowing that if they say "Hey, you, come here!" the toddler will only run all the faster, in order to prolong the game of "chase." These are people who need their sleep, and many of them nap right along with their toddlers. These are people who may *feel* much older than their chronologic age because they are putting out so much physical energy each day. It's only fair to give them the assurance that they aren't really getting much older—only their children are changing over time. Perhaps maxim #2 will encourage them to see themselves as a reflection of a timeless and unchanging God, too.

*3. The eyes in the back of a parent's head are usually equal in potency to any exploration a toddler can try.* This maxim is another one that is intended to reassure parents that they are up to the task at hand. This one even comes with its own scientific (sort of) formula:

$$\text{Efficacy of the occipital eyes} = \frac{(\textit{Suspicion Index})(\textit{Age of Parent})(\textit{Experience})}{\text{Anxiety Quotient}}$$

For those who have extreme math anxiety, let me put it this way. If your index of suspicion goes up easily ("It's been quiet in there for a good four minutes. I wonder what's going on?"), or if you are an older parent (possibly more experienced at doing multiple things at once), *or* if you are a more experienced parent with, say, four children rather than one, the efficacy of those eyes in the back of your head is likely to go *up.*

If, on the other hand, you have a great deal of anxiety about how well you are doing as the parent of a toddler, the efficacy of those eyes in the back of your head is likely to go *down*—you won't be as likely to trust your own intuition as to when to check on your little darling, and therefore you're likely to check on her every minute unnecessarily. So trust the eyes in the back of your head to do what they can for you—you'll be more efficient in the long run.

*4. Second babies bounce well.* For a majority of families, if the toddler is the number one child, chances are fair that a number two child will come along during the first child's second or third year of life. This maxim is designed to remind parents that they needn't be terribly anxious about their number two child's safety around number one, because second babies seem to roll with the punches quite easily.

When number one picks up number two out of the infant seat and attempts to carry her across the room, dropping her instead on the living room carpet, a parent can recite "second babies bounce well" and know that no irreparable damage has been done.

The majority of number two babies seem to be easy, roll-with-the-punches type folks. They go along with the family schedule (studies have shown that they spend significantly more time in the family car than a first child does in infancy). They maintain a buoyant, happy demeanor in the face of all kinds of challenges. They adjust well psychologically to various situations. It is as if on the way out of the birth canal they read the book that says "you must be flexible at all times, in all circumstances."

This maxim is also intended to reassure the new parent-of-two that second-borns *do* get as much stimulation as number one babies, even if parents don't have the same amount of time to spend with them. Number two child will get part of her stimulation and information about the world around her from number one, as well as from any parental input.

If you are the parent of two children, you probably know by now that the number one child can elicit a smile and a laugh from number two when not even parents can. Second babies bounce well—they are survivors and tend to be what parents term "easy babies" in their demeanor. How much of this can be attributed to the fact that parents are much more relaxed the second time around? I don't think anybody but God knows the answer to that one.

5. *Things change.* Your child is undergoing a process of change with each passing month of life—new skills, new cognitive abilities, new language options. You saw it in infancy, and now you can see it once again in the toddler years.

Your child is *in process.* Sometimes you enjoy the process, some days you'd rather not participate in that process, and on a few selected days you wish the process had never begun at all. But your child is definitely in a process that you hope will result in a well-rounded, confident, and socially-skilled human being who has an ongoing relationship with the Lord of all life.

On the days in which you think you can't possibly take one more minute of policing your toddler—remind yourself that things change. Your child *will* outgrow this stage of life. Your child will mature, learn to be a good decision-maker, and learn to laugh at her own mistakes (especially if her parents know how!).

You will look back on this stage of life some day and remember when you thought you had reached the end of your rope. Only the grace of God kept you hanging on. It's a gift, really, to come to the point of realizing that only God can help us through. Isn't that what trusting the love of God is all about?

Let's move forward into the toddler years with confidence, a sense of wonder, and a sense of *humor.* After all, God found the toddler years important enough to live them himself, in the form of Jesus Christ.

While we don't know what Jesus' development was like, it's possible that as a real human child he experienced the high-energy phases, the giggling fits, the *no* stage, the questions, and the climb-everywhere stage, just as any toddler does. These phases may seem to be rebellious but they are primarily a reflection of the child learning to separate from the parent. God puts up with each of us as we "toddle" and learn to stand and walk in our faith. Surely we can do the same for our toddlers, who are also children of a great and glorious God.

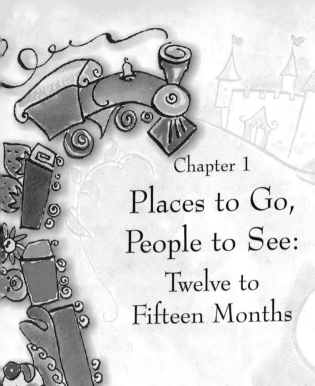

# Chapter 1

# Places to Go, People to See:
## Twelve to Fifteen Months

So, your cute and adorable infant, the child who so placidly lay on a blanket on the floor and was *still where you put him* when you returned from the bathroom sixty seconds later, that child is placid—and immobile—no longer. Your toddler, whether crawling, walking, cruising the furniture, or heading across the backyard at a full run, is now *mobile*—"a going concern." He delights in this new skill, sometimes bursting into coos of delight or outrageous peals of laughter simply because he can *move*. What has happened?

## Large Motor Skills: Steps of Faith

Walking involves a whole series of motor skills put together into a fluid motion, and these skills are not easy to master. Babies attempt them at very different rates of "risk," dependent on temperament and personality traits, birth order in the family unit, and anatomical, metabolical, and psychological make-up.

In order to allow the torso to balance on the pelvic girdle, humans must tighten up the muscles of the lower back, primarily the dorsi muscles that create the "curve" to our waistline and upper thighs. All of these muscles have to be strengthened to the point that they can hold the weight of the body while allowing ease of movement in any direction. Your toddler has been tightening these muscle groups for the past six months or so through sitting, crawling, pulling to a stand, cruising the furniture, and finally, taking that first big step without arm support.

Next, the infant has to develop a proprioceptive sense—that is, the ability to know in time and space where the feet and legs are without looking at them. This he may have done quite well through crawling (remember when he used to get that back leg caught while moving from a sitting to a crawling position?), but the process has to continue once your child decides on the upright posture for the majority of his movements. The nerves and central nervous system (CNS) must once again do a finely honed dance, now taking gravity into account in a new way—voilà, in walking, the legs are always *under* the torso, not behind the torso or to the side of it. This requires new sensory input, which eventually becomes so automatic that we don't think about it at all.

This proprioceptive sense is one of the most difficult things for adults to regain if they must relearn to walk. The sensory nerves are put together early on in one's life, and it takes significant training for them to relearn the skill of locomotion in the adult years. There is a window of time for these nerve endings, much like the window of time in which language acquisition is easiest for humans.

After this sense of space is developed, the muscles of the legs need to be strengthened and taught the sequence of events that leads to human locomotion. The walker must, in specific sequence, pick up a foot, swing it through an arc to plant the heel in front of him, then roll the weight from heel to toe on that foot, and, while balancing the weight on the ball of that foot, begin the process all over again on the opposite side, shifting body weight slightly from side to side as well as from back to front (assuming one is walking in a forward direction).

### Step to it

Anyone who has watched a toddler walk will tell you that the fine points of weight-shift from the back to the front of the foot are lost in the early efforts. The toddler basically picks up the entire foot and "slaps" it onto the floor again, primarily using the muscles of the upper leg to lift the foot. The subtle shift of body-weight from side to side and the even more subtle shift of weight from the back of the foot to the front of the foot will come later. Both of these shifts, incidentally, utilize relatively fine movement of muscles around the ankle. We will come back to this later.

Eventually, the child will be able to walk *in the direction he has decided to go* and stop to look at something on a table, or even pick up something from the floor. To pick up an object, the child will bend the knees while still standing, shift his body weight to accommodate the change in posture of the upper body, straighten his legs, raise the torso once again, and continue walking

27

in the same direction as before, or change direction to walk to a new thing or person.

When you see your toddler begin to move from object to object in what seems to be a very haphazard fashion, remember that he is practicing all of these skills. Whereas an adult moves methodically around the room, looking at pictures on the wall for instance, a toddler may dart back and forth across a room, retracing his steps a dozen times and going from object to object. This is an attempt to learn exactly what it's like to walk from the sofa to the coffee table, or how to maneuver from the chair to the lamp. He may repeat this journey a dozen times a day, with different objects in his hands or wearing something different. (How many times has your toddler gotten away from you during a diaper change and madly rushed around the room until you could capture that cute little body in order to diaper it again?) Perhaps his adventures will take place with different folks around, or with (and then without) the cat in the room.

> ***That* is why your house looks like a vicious tornado hit— your toddler has performed exciting experiments all day long!**

All of these are variations on a theme, and in the toddler's mind they must *each* be tried. *That* is why your house looks like a vicious tornado hit by the end of every day—your toddler has performed a series of very scientific and exciting experiments all day long! (Do you recall what the Absent-Minded Professor's laboratory looked like? Experiments are rarely tidy.)

Keep in mind that all of us as babies had to try similar experiments in order to learn our environments. You yourself had the Absent-Minded Professor's laboratory! Perhaps having that understanding will allow you to be more motivated to work at the forgiveness that a parent of a toddler needs each day. Come to think of it, the forgiveness that every parent must extend on a daily basis is a kind of *grace.* Think about God's parenting style with us. Are you reflecting his grace in your own family relationships?

### Eyes on the prize

What can we learn from the first walking efforts of the toddler? As he masters the sequence of skills necessary for walking, the toddler pays no conscious attention to what he's doing. He only focuses on *where he wishes to go.* He pays no heed to the mechanics of the complex skills he's about, nor does he sit and worry over whether he'll be able to do the skills, how much effort it might take, or whether that effort might be better expended somewhere else. The toddler sets his sights on the goal and puts everything he has into that effort to get there.

Rarely do we see in adult life the kind of single-minded determination that a toddler exhibits in learning to walk. What would the church—and the world—be like if every human being were that single-minded in following God? In learning to do God's will in every one of life's situations? The world would be a different place.

And watch the toddler's head and eyes as he learns to walk. Where are his eyes focused? Not on his feet and legs, but on the face of the one to whom he walks. His successes, his failures, his falls are all entrusted to the face of the parent to whom he toddles. The toddler even takes his cues about success and failure from the parent. If a toddler suddenly falls to a sitting position, he will usually contemplate the parent's face and demeanor for a moment before deciding whether to cry or not. By laughing, smiling, or talking to the toddler, a parent can often convince the child that the fall wasn't too bad, no harm done, and he should try again.

> **Rarely do we see in adult life the kind of single-minded determination that a toddler exhibits in learning to walk.**

If toddlers learning to walk put that much faith in the parent, why is it that adults put so little faith in the God of all creation as we learn to walk, run, or crawl to the throne of grace? If you want to see absolute unselfconscious faith in action, watch a toddler take his first—or his hundred-and-first—step.

## Small Motor Skills: Aren't Opposable Thumbs *Great?*

We've seen that the toddler is intently involved with one

of the most basic of human skills—the large motor skill of walking. But that doesn't mean that he has ignored the other skill-groups. A child at twelve to fifteen months of age can now improve his manual dexterity with small objects in all kinds of ways. The same pattern of nerve-and-muscle-coordination that occurs in walking takes place in the development of small motor skills. The proximal muscle groups, which are closer to the center of the body—closer to the brain, if you will—develop skills before the distal muscle groups, which are farther away from the brain.

The infant began by vaguely waving the arms in space, then developed the ability to hit an object in front of his eyes, then used the fingers to grab an object (Mom's hair? Dad's tie?) with a rake-like motion of the four fingers together. Then came the skill of picking up an object using the index finger and the thumb together to press the object between those two digits. (This is known as the *pincer grasp.*)

Now, the toddler refines the movements of the fingers and the hand even further by practicing picking up objects between the thumb and the *other* fingers of the hand. You will see your toddler pick up objects with the thumb and each finger in succession on some days. These are the days when he stands at the side of the coffee table, picking up magazines and dropping them onto the floor over and over again. He is probably using a slightly different grasp for each drop. You will also see him coordinate the movements of the thumb against all four fingers together, in order to pick up larger objects. He is learning the usefulness of the opposable thumb.

The opposable thumb is one of the things (by no means the *only* thing) that makes us different from the great apes in the eyes of anthropologists and biologists. If you have ever seen a picture of the hands of the orangutan, the gorilla, the chimpanzee, and the human together, you will note that the human hand is the only one in which the thumb can be rotated (using the muscles of the *thenar eminence*) into the palm of the hand. All of the great apes have thumbs, but they are either rudimentary (as in the orangutan) or able to rotate toward the hand but not actually meet the other fingers across the palm (as in the gorilla and chimpanzee).

> **You will see your toddler pick up objects with the thumb and each finger in succession.**

If you study your own hand for a moment, you can see how very useful it is for the thumb to meet the other fingers across the palm of the hand. It enables us to carry things in a variety of ways, to manipulate objects, and to perform fine motor skills such as holding a paintbrush or playing a musical instrument. The entire sensory system of the hand allows us to sense hot and cold, velvet and wool, rough and smooth. Add this ability to the myriad of possibilities for grasp, and you realize that, without a doubt, the human hand is truly a miracle all by itself.

So, you will see the twelve- to fifteenth-month-old child checking out his hands at all times of the day, in all substances (dog food is no exception!), with all possible solid objects and with some that are impossible—ever tried to pick up regular old Jello? How about bathwater? Your toddler will attempt to pick up these and thousands of other objects in the world around him, all using differing positions of that wonderful thumb.

### The value of opposites

How like God it is to use even our opposable thumbs to teach us truth. From our opposable thumbs we understand the value of opposition. Sometimes tension, even between people, can be constructive and creative. If we all thought alike—went in the same direction—the world would quickly become a very boring place.

We can compare and contrast the left-brain and right-brain people of the world and be in dialogue with those who see things in a diametrically opposite way to our own view. In the New Testament, Jesus never once *refused* to talk with someone he disagreed with. He was always open to a dialogue, to listening to someone else's point of view, or to discussing ideas over dinner even if the social majority didn't approve of his dinner host.

The church, too, is a wondrous conglomerate of personalities, needs, learning styles, types of intelligence, visions, and dreams. How can we be open to different points of view among such varied personalities? How can we keep the dialogue going, to the glory of God? We can begin by returning to the basics of our faith, remembering that Christianity is not a set of rules and regulations, but an ongoing relationship with the God of laughter, mercy, and love. We can begin by watching a toddler learn to use his thumb and finger to pick up a block from the floor.

# Social Skills: Send in the Clowns!

The twelve- to fifteen-month-old toddler is a delightful creature, full of wonder and fun. This age group seems willing to share humor with adults in a fairly unself-conscious fashion. For the most part, a twelve to fifteen month old will clap hands, play the "so big" game by throwing the hands up over the head, wave bye-bye, and even dance for strangers, as long as a parent is around to witness the action too.

### *Perfect strangers*
This is in distinct contrast to the nine- to twelve-month-old infant, who will generally have some degree of "stranger anxiety" that inhibits his behavior in front of unfamiliar people. The early toddler will, with little provocation, bounce up and down on his feet to a beat or to music in the mall, smile and laugh at a stranger, or even accept an object from the stranger's hand—again, as long as there is a parent around to cling to in case things get too risky. He may beat his hand against the surface of a chair or a sofa while squealing with delight at his own prowess. If the stranger witnessing this should beat a hand against the sofa or squeal along with the toddler, so much the better. In terms of social inter-actions, the twelve- to fifteen-month-old toddler is, truly, the stuff that clowns are made of.

> **The toddler is, truly, the stuff that clowns are made of.**

Why is this new confidence in social skills growing? As with everything else about human development, there are a number of factors that come into play here. Usually by this age, the child has had several months of experience with "strangers," most of whom are actually known to the child or to his parents. So he has a backlog of experience that tells him that other people can be safe, even fun. In addition, a toddler has more physical confidence in his ability to get away from a stranger, now that he can walk or even run.

The child also appears to have a new sense of himself and a budding sense of humor. Granted, the "humor" is defined entirely by the toddler—the child who is bouncing up and down to music may burst into peals of laughter and expect the stranger to do the same. But still, it is an early experiment in social behavior. If parents have smiled and applauded these efforts in the home, the twelve- to fifteen-month-old toddler will usually feel it is safe to try them out on someone who has rarely, or never, been in the home situation, and wait to see what the stranger will do. If the stranger smiles, applauds, or even goes so far as to *imitate* the toddler's behavior (dancing with him, squealing, nodding his head when the toddler does, etc.), the toddler will generally continue or escalate the behavior—sometimes to the chagrin of the parent.

But it's all part of the big experiment, to see whether the toddler can entice a much larger human (i.e., an older child or an adult) into following the toddler's lead. This is social power at its best! To be able to walk into a situation with adults, besides the parents, and interrupt an adult conversation while quickly maneuvering into the spotlight is an extremely powerful game. Even if one has to perform outrageous behavior in order to manipulate the adults in the room, the power to manipulate adults is seductive enough to ensure that the toddler will give it a try.

### Seeking approval and attention

I think there is also an element of approval that dictates the twelve- to fifteen-month-old toddler's behavior in social circumstances. The toddler wants to know that he is approved of in a social setting, just as we all want to know that others approve of us. (The cosmetics and fashion industries are built upon this very need for approval!) The child needs occasional approval from strangers, but his biggest need for approval at this stage is from his parents. So he will dance and coo and wave his arms around in front of a stranger, attempting to draw all the adults in the room into his brand of fun, but always keeping a watchful eye out for the approval of the parent.

Many of the parents I meet in my pediatric practice are concerned about when to let the child have the spotlight. I tell them that at this stage of life, when you are with close friends or family and your toddler decides to play the clown, let him do it. Let him be center stage for a few moments. Laugh and applaud his antics, and give him big hugs to say "I love you and you did a great job." You are helping him see himself as separate from you, as an individual who can be applauded in his own right, and as someone of whom you are proud. It's the same show of support as attending the school play he is in, going to the band concert when his band performs, cheering at the soccer game when his team plays. It's an overall attitude of approval and unconditional love that your child needs to know is there for him, at any age.

## God's unique children

How can we see the hand of God in the toddler who seeks to be the clown? By looking in the mirror and recognizing that we *all* need approval—from other people as well as from God. This need for approval waxes and wanes throughout our lives as we move through the varying phases of human development. Our own stage of development is unique to us. Any one of our fellow human beings may be in an entirely different stage, with different needs and different insights.

The toddler-clown scenario also reflects the value of *humor* as a mode of human interaction. Often in the church, we have a rather somber mentality, as if a darker, always-serious mindset is what God expects of us. Laughter is foreign to many worship services I have attended. Expressions of *joy* as well as respect during a communion service, for instance, may be seen as inappropriate in some churches.

> **The toddler-clown, anxious for approval, never forgets who his audience is.**

While it is important to recognize the suffering of Christ on the cross, what about the Resurrection? What about the Good News that life overcomes death, that good ultimately banishes evil? And what about this idea of the Eucharist as "feast"? Many Christians can become so focused on the task at hand that we completely miss the joy and the humor that God offers us in the midst of our struggles. We can miss the fact that Jesus, as a reflection of the Father's joy, undoubtedly had a sense of humor and laughed often. We can sing the words to songs like "Lord of the Dance" but miss the joy that comes from dancing with the Lord of Life. The toddler-clown, on the other hand, doesn't miss the joy of life for a moment.

### Our holy cheering section

One other point that the toddler-clown shows us: the toddler, in all of his attention-seeking antics, relies heavily on the presence of the parent for comfort and approval. The child is constantly alert to any reaction from the watching parent.

Do we do the same? Are we aware of the presence of God throughout most of our days, or do we only think about God on Sunday mornings—or not even then? When we go through a difficult time at the office or at home with our children, do we remember that God is the loving parent present with us in the room, observing all that we do and cheering us on in our daily lives? Or do we forget which audience we are playing to?

The toddler-clown, anxious for approval, never forgets who his audience is. He does everything he can to please the beloved parent. May we, as adults, learn to have such authentic, unself-conscious awareness of God in all that we do at work or play.

# Language and Communication Skills: A Few Choice Words

The twelve- to fifteen-month-old child has much to

say—and a very incomplete ability to say it! He literally can babble on for hours while playing, and only a very few words, if any, are intelligible to the listener. He uses inflection and intonation much like that which he hears. The toddler who raises his voice sharply at his stuffed animals and who yells as he plays by himself is probably hearing those vocal tones from others in the household. Imitation is his key learning tool here, so it behooves parents to use both tone and vocabulary that they won't mind their toddler emulating in a public place.

### Acquiring language

At around eight months of age, the human infant is capable of making every sound used in every language in the world. Only some of these sounds are reinforced by the infant's environment, and by twelve months of age the child has dropped the sounds that he doesn't hear in the language(s) around him.

> **The twelve to fifteen month old will use a jargon filled with the intonations of his "native tongue."**

So the twelve to fifteen month old will use a jargon filled with the intonations and the sounds of his "native tongue"—the French-speaking infants will drop what English speakers think of as the "th" sound, the English-speaking infants will drop the clicking sounds heard only in the Bushmen languages, the Spanish-speaking infants will no longer make the American "r" sound, and the infants who hear Chinese languages will pay careful attention to the tones and pitches that are used to differentiate words. The brain circuitry used to create and sustain language is indeed one of our greatest gifts as human beings.

The twelve- to fifteen-month-old child plays happily on the floor with toys, or more likely rushes from place to place with a toy in each hand, babbling to himself as he goes. There will probably be a "Mama" or a "Dada" in there somewhere, along with a "baba," a "bubba," or something that might indicate a sibling, the family cat, or a favorite toy. But there may not be much more than that, certainly not anything that a stranger would recognize as a word.

The toddler now has an inkling that a word is a discrete symbol for a single object or action. As an infant, he may have delighted in being carried around the room so he could point to objects and be told the name of each object by a parent. Now he carries the process one step further and attempts to express the idea with his own version of the word.

Most toddlers at this stage understand that "Mama" is not all adults, nor all females, nor all people who feed him, but his own mother. The word "Dada" or "Papa" refers not to all males, but to his own father. At this stage, the toddler may say "Dada" all day long, as long as things are going well. However, when he falls and hurts himself, needs a pants-change, or needs comfort in some other way, most toddlers will switch to the use of the word "Mama."

Why "Mama" usually is used for comfort and

"Dada" for the status quo is not clear. I have wondered whether it has to do with the fact that mothers, for the most part, instinctively play with infants by cuddling and drawing them close to the body, while many dads play with infants by holding them out away from the body, tossing the child in the air, or making him "fly." So in a time of real distress, whatever the nature of the distress, "Mama" is who to call because she will provide a hug and reassurance, while "Dada" reflects more active, motion-oriented activity.

Both images of parenting and parental caring are needed in the life of the child. Both words will usually be used in the course of a day. Both parents, and the unique ways in which they express their love for the child, are crucial for the child's development and well-being.

### Calling God's name

How do these few words of the early toddler recall the loving nature of God? How wonderful it is that the child learns to call on the most fundamental of relationships in his life first! If a child's first few words were representative only of random objects he sees on a daily basis, the child might well use "TV" or the name of a neighbor's dog as his first words. But the child almost always uses "Mama" and "Dada" before other words. Even if those are not the *first* utterances, certainly they are the most common sounds by fifteen months.

I believe this reflects the importance of relationships for human beings. We were created to be in relationship with God the Creator, the Redeemer and Sustainer of all life. We find throughout our lives that healthy relationships bring us more joy and fulfillment than mere *things* can ever give. The early toddler reflects this knowledge in his use of "Mama" and "Dada" as his first routine utterances. He knows, and learns to speak first, the names of love and support in his life.

How often, as we go through our adult days, do we speak the name of God? Do we do so with reverence, with familiarity, with joy? Or do we use that name as a social (rather inane, actually) expression, as in "Oh, my God!" when we're not really thinking of God at all?

> **How wonderful it is that the child learns to call on the most fundamental of relationships in his life first!**

Ideally, the toddler lives in the knowledge that his parent is always there, always listening, always caring, and ready to be supportive as the toddler goes about the business of learning his world. Later, he will learn the words to express complex ideas and feelings. For now, it is enough to speak the name of Love.

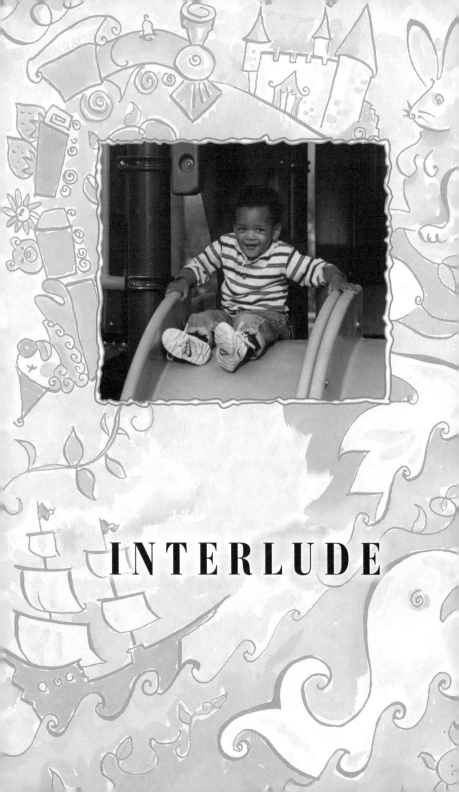

# INTERLUDE

# On the Nature of Gravity

*The spiritual journey is one of continually falling on your face, getting up, brushing yourself off, looking sheepishly at God, and taking another step.*
—Sri Aurobindo, Christian mystic

We watch toddlers pull to a stand against furniture or a friendly human leg. We watch them tip and flail. We watch them learn the use of their arms as ancillary balancing tools. We see them flop to the ground after a single tentative step, looking either surprised, happy with themselves for having made the effort, or as though their dignity has been injured and they are just waiting for an audience before bursting into wails of grief and despair. All of these things we know will happen, and the reason that we *know* they will happen is the gravitational pull of the earth's mass on our bodies—what we call gravity. We take it for granted.

Scientists have studied astronauts for over four decades, hoping to learn more about the effects of a gravity-free environment on the human body. What they have learned so far is not surprising: human physiology is specifically designed to work best in a gravity field such as ours here on earth.

### Wonderfully made

Our esophagus is muscled in order to move swallowed solids and liquids from our mouths into our stomachs— but those muscles are much more efficient when helped along by gravity (otherwise, why have the mouth *higher* than the stomach?). Yes, it *is* possible to swallow while standing on one's head, but it's a lot more comfortable to swallow when gravity is there to help, as any hospital patient will tell you. You will notice that most bedridden patients prefer to sit up as much as possible when attempting to swallow something. That's because our entire muscle system is geared to work with gravity.

The human circulatory system is certainly geared to function in the presence of gravity. Major arteries coming right off the heart—the pump for the entire system—go straight to the head to supply the brain with oxygenated blood before the strong push of the blood mass is lost in the myriad of smaller vessels and capillary beds. Muscles in the walls of the veins in the lower legs are stronger than elsewhere because they have the hardest "pushing" to do of any veins in the human body. They have to push a continuous column of deoxygenated blood straight *up* against gravity, to get it back to the heart so it can be reoxygenated and sent around again.

Our intestinal systems are packed in such a way and with appropriate "padding" in the form of fat that we can maintain an upright posture against gravity, either standing or sitting, and not have our intestines fall out or fall down too far. We have stiffer cartilage in our external ears than anywhere else on our bodies because cartilage can hold its shape against gravity. This keeps our ears in a position to capture sound waves from multiple directions, allowing us to hear. We can breathe deeply because the diaphragm, the large sheet of muscle at the base of our lungs, is stretched across the bottom of the thorax in such a way that gravity aids its stretch, allowing our lungs to attain maximum filling capacity. (Have you noticed that when people "stand up and stretch," they generally swing their arms out away from the chest and take a deep breath? That's allowing maximum stretch of the diaphragm muscle, too, in conjunction with gravity.)

### *Boom!*

So it's clear from human physiology that we are designed to live in an environment of gravity, exactly geared to the gravitational pull of the earth's mass on our bodies. The average toddler is busy figuring this out on a daily basis. You will see the twelve- to eighteen-month-old child learning to stand against the pull of gravity, but he doesn't stop there! Next the toddler learns to walk with an object in the hands—both hands together at first, and then an object in each hand. After that, he spends most of every day exploring the wonders of gravity—carrying objects, dropping them in different places, picking up different objects, dropping *those* in different places.

He throws things down and watches where they land, what noises they make upon landing, whether they still look familiar on the floor, whether they land right-side-up or upside-down (which is, in itself, a gravity-dictated concept). He tosses objects *up,* only to watch them fall toward earth again. He learns about textures, mass, air resistance, the nature of materials (plastic lands differently than crystal does), and the nature of his own body by watching these objects land and by watching how *he* lands when he falls. Most toddlers, well after they have accomplished walking, go through a stage where they intentionally fling themselves toward the floor, just to see what will happen. The toddler learns that, no matter how many times he throws an object *up,* it will eventually fall *down.* (The exception to this is the helium balloon, which falls *up* when someone lets go of it—and many toddlers are upset by, or even afraid of, helium balloons precisely because the balloons defy the law of gravity!)

Once again, we can see determination in action as the toddler studies *every*thing in his path in the light of this new knowledge of gravity. By the time we are adults, we are so accustomed to gravitational pull from the earth that we rarely think about it until we are once again reminded of its wonders by a toddler. Meanwhile, the child has learned an important lesson in *faith*—faith that gravity will always be there, that its effects will be the same tomorrow as they were today, that this mysterious pull back to earth will affect *all* objects and all people, not just some materials and selected individuals.

### God's sustaining love
But isn't gravity more than just a condition of our existence on earth? Can't it also be a constant reminder of the love of God? We don't always *see* God's love, but we see its effects. We don't have to *think* about it for it

to be present with us.

Some of us take God's love for granted and are no longer captivated by its wonders. We need to take a lesson from toddlers and go about studying that love with a determination that says "our lives depend on it." We need to be *aware* of God's presence in the world around us. We need to try everything in our lives against that gold standard of unconditional love, just as the toddler judges every action against the constant presence of gravity. Throwing away our untested and unexamined notions about life, we need instead to test and examine our lives as expressions of God's love. As Paul said, "when I was a child, I saw as a child, I thought as a child. Now that I am an adult, I see things in a different way" (my translation from the Greek).

Isn't *this* what "growing in the faith" means, this constant examination and application of God's grace and mercy in our own lives? Growing in the faith can even mean re-examining our own childhoods, discerning the "old tapes" of unconscious motivations and preconceived notions that developed as children, and trying *those* out against the gold standard of God's love. Father Thomas Keating, in his book *Contemplative Prayer,* says that he believes that maturing in the faith is a lifelong process of examining these old assumptions and habits, usually held from early childhood, and of holding these premises and habits up to the light of God's grace in order to make each of them consistent in thought, word, and deed with the love of God. It's a lifelong process and sometimes it's painful as well as stretching. But if the average toddler can stretch and grow in his knowledge of the world around him by studying gravity and its effects, we can learn to stretch and grow in our knowledge of God's love, can't we? (If we ever feel *guilty* for studying God's love, we can remember the intensity and freedom with which toddlers study gravity!)

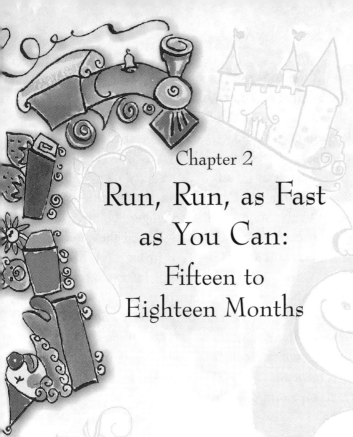

## Chapter 2

# Run, Run, as Fast as You Can:

## Fifteen to Eighteen Months

The fifteen- to eighteen-month-old child is more purposeful, more confident, more intentional than she was at twelve months of age. She has spent countless hours exploring the environment(s) around her, she has gleaned information through the school of "hard knocks," she has welcomed learning with open arms. What are you, the parent of this whirling dervish, likely to see in the months ahead?

## Large Motor Skills: Running the Race

With very few exceptions, the fifteen-month-old toddler has learned to walk (if your fifteen month old does *not* walk, be sure to mention it to your pediatrician). She can now lift the foot and place it again without looking at the foot, and she is much more accurate in the placement. She doesn't *slap* the foot down on the floor, but actually begins to use a bit of flexion at the ankle to place each step. The stance is still wide-based (meaning the toes point out at a forty-five to sixty degree angle from the direction she's going), but not as wide-based as it was at twelve months. She no longer "bounces" on the hip with each step, but has tightened the gluteus and the pelvic muscles to solidly shift her body weight from side to side. All in all, the skill of walking is becoming less of a conscious effort for her.

You may notice two other things about your child's locomotion at this stage of life: 1) she begins sometime between fifteen and eighteen months to experiment with walking *backwards,* and 2) she picks up the pace of walking to the point of a "trot" at times.

### New ways to move

Walking backwards is often accomplished first as an unconscious action, in reaction to some startling event occurring in front of her eyes. For instance, the toddler instinctively moves backwards when a strange dog approaches, when a parent raises a voice with a loud *no* as she walks towards the fire in the fireplace, or when she is startled by someone coming through a doorway. After several times of instinctively moving backwards while on her feet, she will try to replicate this action at will.

Walking backwards is basically a reverse of forward locomotion: the toddler picks up the foot toes first, balancing body weight on one side while planting the contralateral foot *behind* the body, heel-to-toes, then shifting the body weight to that side while repeating the movement on the other side.

> **Walking backwards is often accomplished first as an unconscious action.**

Toddlers can be seen to shift weight clumsily while backward-walking, which results in a gait that lumbers from side to side in a comic fashion. (Adults, incidently, pick up the foot heel first to walk backwards, using the toes as a bit of extra spring with each step. This propels them more firmly in the backwards direction and decreases the side-to-side lumbering appearance to the gait). Nonetheless, the child arrives where she wishes to go, which delights her to no end. In particular, toys on a string that can be pulled backwards while the toddler walks backwards will delight the heart of most fifteen month olds.

In addition to being able to pull a toy on a string, the ability to walk backwards allows the toddler to study a whole range of sights from a different perspective. She now sees *where she's been* rather than where she's going, and this idea alone may be worth days of walking backwards for the fifteen to eighteen month old. Often a toddler this age will walk backwards for a bit, then stand still, turning the head around to see what's behind her (where she's going), smile or laugh, and then begin walking once again, only to see the same objects three steps later from the opposite perspective. Parents need to be prepared for the child to bump into many objects in the home as the child pursues this exciting task. She isn't really failing to watch where she's going, she's *very* aware of where she's going. She merely wishes to study the objects in her surrounding environment from a different perspective as she progresses around the room.

### Catch me if you can

The other aspect of locomotion that the fifteen- to eighteen-month-old toddler achieves is the ability to *run.* Any parent who has ever chased a toddler down a hallway in the doctor's office, across the sanctuary after (or during!) a church service, or down the corridors of a shopping mall, can tell you that toddlers can *run,* and run *fast.* They particularly delight in being called by the parent or caregiver, and then taking off running in exactly the *opposite* direction—this is in order to be *chased* by the adult. Most toddlers will crow with delight as they take off, or at least smile as they run.

> **Toddlers delight in being called and then taking off in the *opposite* direction.**

Running differs from walking in pace as well as in gait. Of course the distance the toddler goes is covered in a shorter period of time by running than by walking, using more steps per minute. But the distance covered per step is also different in running. We tend to cover more distance per step when running than we do in walking, and this again has to do with gravity, acceleration, and force.

When we walk, we generate a small amount of forward momentum with each step. When we *run,* we generate a much larger amount of forward momentum with each stride, which literally carries us further with each step we take. In addition, older children and adults tend to use the arms for significant counterbalance as they run, which again helps carry the body in a forward direction with each stride. This forward momentum not only carries us in the direction we are trying to go, it smooths out the motion of running and markedly decreases the side-to-side swaying that most human beings generate as they walk. The end result? Much more efficient movement through the environment with less expenditure of energy per foot of space covered.

The toddler very quickly realizes this fact and utilizes it on a daily basis. No longer does she walk from place to place, she literally *runs* everywhere she goes. This stage is hard for adults to keep pace with, and many caregivers need an afternoon nap as much or more than the toddler does!

The skills of walking, walking backwards, and running are extremely useful for adults as well as for toddlers, though adults are often not aware of using these skills. (Try maneuvering a grocery cart through the grocery store without walking backwards at least *once!*) But the toddler is aware of them and delights in her prowess.

### A fresh perspective

The toddler who walks or runs backwards sees her world in new ways. She reminds us to keep learning to look at things from different perspectives. Jesus had the gift of really *listening* to what other people were saying. He could put himself in their place, walking backwards with them, if you will, to see their environment from a new and different angle.

For instance, Jesus honored the woman's request to heal her daughter after she responded to him *from her own perspective.* She told him, "Yes, Lord, but even the dogs under the table eat the children's crumbs" (see Mark 7:25-30). She spoke as one of the "dogs under the table," that is, not of Jewish heritage. If Jesus modeled such openness to seeing the world in different ways, how can we miss the message—especially when our toddler is showing us the same thing, every time she walks backwards?

### Running to grace

The image of running can also be applied to our spiritual life. When we *run,* we go toward the goal in an energy-efficient fashion. When we walk, we expend extra energy in the side-to-side movement. Toddlers learn this quickly and use running to their advantage to *get to the goal.* By analogy, the more single-minded we are in becoming the imitation of Christ, the more we *run* toward the throne of grace and the more efficiently we arrive at our goal. We can use our spiritual energies in a whole-hearted way to move toward Love, and we will be greeted by the open arms of our heavenly Parent. That's a goal worth running toward!

**The more single-minded we are in becoming the imitation of Christ, the more we *run* toward the throne of grace.**

## Small Motor Skills: The Relationship of Two Objects to Each Other

While the fifteen- to eighteen-month-old toddler is busy with large motor skills, she has by no means dropped interest in the small motor skills. She is fascinated with movement of the hands in all forms and will sometimes walk around staring at her own hands or those of another person as she goes. She will, as we have seen, spend the majority of each day walking around with an object in each hand, perhaps dropping things in every room in the house just to see if they fall *down.* As soon as one hand is empty, she reaches for another object to carry, and the game goes on. She is comparing the objects she carries for size, texture, color, perhaps taste, weight, noise-as-it-drops, and several other parameters.

Although the comparison of the "intrinsic" qualities of the objects are totally fascinating for the twelve to fifteen month old, for the fifteen to eighteen month old, new areas of mental activity are opening up. The fifteen month old wants to explore all the possible relationships of the two objects to each other in time and space.

No longer is "in and out" the wonderful game it was a few months ago. Now the toddler wants to explore *all* the prepositional positions—over, under, around, through, beside, and on top of! She spends large portions of each day manipulating small objects with two hands (at fifteen months) or with a single hand (closer to eighteen months). She carefully places the block over the coffee table, under the newspaper, behind the sofa, and carries it around the sleeping dog (often making three or four complete circles around the dog). All of these activities are improving hand-eye coordination.

She meticulously puts the washcloth on top of the milk carton, only to discover that gravity pulls it to the table top instead. She may try to balance a plastic bottle on top of the houseplant, or her glass of juice on the edge of the plate, just to see if it will stay. In the toddler's mind, the *consequences* of these actions are superfluous. The TV remote-control may be balanced on the coffee table, or on the edge of the plastic laundry basket, or even in the glass of juice, if a parent isn't looking. She is practicing finger control and coordination with every experiment—how *do* you hold onto the cellular phone until it's completely submerged in the bathtub? These and many other burning questions are pursued with vigor and enthusiasm each day.

Not to be outdone by small objects, she may also use her own body to explore "over, under, around, and through." Suddenly she's on top of the coffee table; she's under the dining room chair; she's beside the TV. We begin to see the toddler's cognitive development pulling her large and small motor skills closer together in daily activity. She climbs onto the sofa while holding a block in each hand at the same time—quite a sophisticated action for someone who a year ago couldn't even roll over, let alone grasp objects!

## A place for everything

So, your toddler begins to be intrigued by the relationship of two objects with each other—which includes blocks and a container. But now she's not content to merely place the blocks in the container—she is mesmerized by putting the round block in the round hole, the triangular block in the triangle hole, the star-shaped block in the star-shaped hole. This reflects not only her facility with two objects and their potential relationships, but it tells us that she is starting to notice that objects may have different shapes. She has probably traced the shape of many different objects with her fingers and/or her hands up until now, and now she begins to make good use of that knowledge.

> **She is starting to notice that objects may have different shapes.**

So she may spend all afternoon (between laps around the house, that is) placing shape-sorter blocks into her shape-sorter container, putting all the square blocks in the same place, or putting all the stars on the coffee table and the round ones on the sofa. All of these activities develop visual/spatial awareness as well as small motor skills and are, in essence, self-paced drills for "how-to-recognize-shapes." This spatial recognition will, over time, present itself in the form of simple puzzle-working as well: the car-shaped piece goes in the car-shaped depression in the puzzle-board, the train goes in the train-shaped hole, and so on.

### Faith shapes

These tasks in the realm of what-do-objects-do-in-time-and-space are reminiscent of our life of faith as adults. For instance, don't we start our relationship with God (in much the same way as we begin a romantic relationship) with awareness of minor details? Don't we begin in our Christian faith noticing the "small" things, such as the blazing glory of a sunset or the delighted laughter of a child? Over time, as that relationship with God matures, we become more deeply aware of the shape of the God-shaped hole inside our own souls. We become better able, as we move into a deeper relationship with God, to see the big places where we shut God out, where we don't let him fit.

To draw another parallel, when we pile too many obligations on one another, we are like the toddler stacking blocks that are bound to fall down. We can choose, as adults, to teeter on the edge of life, balancing our roles and responsibilities much as the toddler stacks objects of varying shapes up to the ceiling and watches them fall. Or we can live life intentionally, acknowledging early on that we might need help along the way. We can allow God to take charge of our "juggling act"— our stack of objects and obligations, our heart, mind, and will. Only when we give over to God all of our life will we be blessed to see the big picture, to view the beautiful scene made up of the small, seemingly meaningless pieces of our existence. Only when we depend on our heavenly Parent to put the puzzle together will all the pieces fit.

# Social Skills: The Center of the Universe

The twelve month old says to herself, "I can move myself." The fifteen month old says to herself, "I can move myself and all my *things.*" The eighteen month old says, "I can move myself and all my *things*—therefore, I run the universe!" If you haven't already begun to see a dictatorial streak in your toddler before fifteen months, don't be surprised to see it surface now. It's there, and (as I often tell parents of toddlers) it's ugly. But it appears to be a necessary stage in human development.

I congratulate toddlers who have thrown a huge tantrum in the grocery store or at the shopping mall because they have hit on the question that remains at the very center of all theological thought: Who *does* run things? Who really *is* in charge of the world, the galaxy, the solar system, the universe(s)? It's a heavy question, one that many religious traditions and philosophies have attempted to deal with over the centuries—and here, in your own kitchen, you have a living reminder of that human pursuit of God.

### This too shall pass
Your toddler may pitch a tantrum when you ask her to get down from the highchair—or, when you attempt to *put* her into the chair. She may squirm out of your grasp as you attempt to get her out of the bathtub—or, she may squirm as you attempt to get her *into* the tub. She

may fall to the floor and roll around, screaming and tearful, as you walk into a store at the mall—or, she may pull the same stunt as you get ready to *leave* the store. There is little predictability regarding specific circumstances here. One day an activity is fun, the next it elicits screams and wails. What's a parent to do?

> **One day an activity is fun, the next it elicits screams and wails.**

I suggest that the first thing a parent should do with a child this age is *stand back emotionally.* Remember that you are not at fault to be asking your child to get out of the chair, to get out of the tub, or to leave the store at closing time. Yours is a reasonable request. Your role as parent has changed from that of nurturing, loving caregiver and supplier of all good things (food, drink, naps, hugs), to the role of nurturing, loving caregiver and *supervisor.* You now supervise, or monitor, your child's behavior and welfare on two fronts: one is safety, the other is social acceptability.

Of course you want your child to be safe, so you *don't* let her run into the street without holding a hand. You don't let her climb out the second story window and hang from the gutters by her arms. You don't let her ride in the car without a safety harness and car seat (*do* you?!). All of these and a hundred other safety issues you pursue in the course of a single day in order to keep your child safe.

By the same token, you monitor your child's social

acceptability on a daily basis. You don't let her yell at the top of her lungs during a worship service. You don't let her bite a friend. You don't let her take her clothes off in public places. You remind her to get her finger out of her nose while talking with Grandma. All these and hundreds of other little social cues you monitor on behalf of your child. It's a tough job, and there are moments when all parents despair that this child will *never* shape up into a real human being—but the children do manage to grow up, with our help.

In truly desperate times, those days when parents feel that they've said no to their toddler three hundred times already and it's only 11 A.M., I suggest that they try dropping back on the social-acceptability-monitoring for a few hours and only monitor the safety issues. It may be a messy day around the house that day, but at least both toddler and parent will have a brief respite from the word no.

### *Minority rule*

The second thing I suggest for parents of toddlers this age, after they step back emotionally from the situation, is to understand that the theme of "I run the universe" is all-pervasive in a toddler's mind. Your toddler will show off for family and friends, perhaps dancing on command or saying "moo" in response to the question "What does the cow say?"—*if* she feels like it. Your request for a show of skills may just as easily fall on deaf ears, unless the toddler thinks it's *her* idea.

Your toddler is suddenly in the business of exploring all the decisions that get made in a day and wondering how she could perform at making every decision. What if *she* set the limits for everything? What if *she* called all the shots for the household? That's the experiment. That is the premise by which she attempts to live, and if you as the parent get in her way, she becomes frustrated and dissolves into tears. (When Jesus talked about being "cast into outer darkness where there is weeping and wailing and gnashing of teeth," I often think of toddler tantrums—they include all of it!)

> **Your toddler has decided that *she* should be in charge—always.**

The toddler really does wish to run everything, if only to find out how bad a job she might do. By the age of two and a half years, most children have happily settled into a routine that allows the parents to make most decisions for the household with little or no protest from the child. But that is precisely because your toddler has done the work of the fifteen to eighteen month old, has looked at who makes the decisions in your family, and has decided that *she* should be in charge—for every decision, always. As you attempt to infuse "adult reality" into her autocratic scheme, there will be sparks and screams. It's just part of the developmental job your toddler is pursuing. The louder she screams, the more she bangs her head against the floor, the better she is doing her job. I know it's a small comfort, if any, but it's all there is to offer at this stage!

As adults we may not bang our head against the floor

when we want control, but we may refuse to turn to God when we want to do something our own way. At these times, we reflect the stubbornness of the toddler who insists on handling things on her own. We tell God we will "do it myself" instead of relying on grace for answers, courage, and strength. Seeing the places where we are assuming too much control, and relinquishing control of those places, is the essence of growth in our relationship with the Almighty.

# INTERLUDE

# Toddler Humor

*To accept the responsibility of being a child of*
*God is to accept the best that life has to offer you.*
—*Stella Terrill Mann, artist*

One of the greatest coping skills that God provides for the parent of a toddler is the gift of humor. Psychologists tell us that humor—the ability to laugh in the midst of a desperate situation—is one of the greatest coping skills that humans have for stressful times. Many survivors of the Holocaust were the people who never forgot how to laugh. In our own country's history, those who survived the Great Depression did so best with the liberal application of humor. Norman Cousins has written about how humor, as an adjunct to medical therapy, helped him recover from a life-threatening illness. Humor is useful for a psychological boost and often for a physiological boost as well.

Harried parents who live with toddlers certainly, in my mind at least, qualify as people who are under siege, leading a stressful life from day to day as they chase their beloved child around a house, an apartment, a shopping mall, a grocery store. The wonderful gift in this stressful time of a parent's life, of course, is *humor*. And often, that humor comes from the toddler herself.

Eighteen-month-old toddlers have the rudiments of humor down, and they will use that humor to stay in the spotlight, no matter what the cost. They will dance at a moment's notice; they will stack blocks, knock them over, and laugh hysterically as they watch the blocks fall all over the family room floor; they will gleefully empty a drawer in the kitchen, climb into the drawer and then laugh—all with the expectation that the adoring adult who is watching will laugh as well.

All of these escapades, in fact, are cleverly designed experiments to see what it is that adults think laughable. Any eighteen month old worth her salt knows that parents are more likely to laugh at her, or with her, if they aren't trying to cook dinner at the same time. Every eighteen month old knows that a "big production" greeting for Dad as he walks through the door in the evening is more likely to put Dad in a mood to play with the toddler, to appreciate her hugs, to laugh at her games. Every toddler knows these things and experiments with the what-can-I-do-to-engage-my-parent-in-an-activity? idea.

### Expect the unexpected

So what exactly *is* humor? Comedians describe humor as "things out of place." Humor involves either physical objects (slapstick humor), plays on words such as puns and "knock-knock" jokes, or mistaken concepts (watch a *Mr. Bean* episode sometime). When a person doesn't expect to see something that suddenly makes an appearance, the usual human response is to laugh (as long as the object that appears isn't threatening to safety). The toddler learns this principle and applies it liberally.

Let's say you are in the grocery store with your toddler. You turn your back to examine the price of cereal. When you turn back three seconds later, your toddler greets you with a big smile—and with the dishcloths you are buying draped over her head. Do you laugh? Probably. This sets up a whole series of variations to be tried. First, and simplest, she will try it again in about fifteen seconds to see if it will elicit a laugh the second time. After about twelve tries, you will say, "OK, that's enough. It was funny the first time, but not now." She learns that repetition of a comedic act has only limited potential to elicit a second, third, or fourth laugh from the parent.

Then she tries variations on the theme—she'll pull her hood up over her eyes. She tries to balance a cereal box on her head. She may even break open the box of sandwich bags to see if those, draped over the head, will make you guffaw once again. Next, she may try to stand up in the grocery cart, putting the dishcloths back over the head, to see if a change of altitude makes Mom laugh. There appears to be no value judgment to these actions and no particular concern for physical safety. She just wants to know what gets your attention, and what gets a laugh. Quickly she learns that attention and laughter may be two entirely different things.

Costume is one of the things that toddler humor focuses on consistently—wearing Dad's shoes, putting on Mom's hat, draping the blanket over the face or neck. Any of these actions might make the parent laugh, if the time is right. With a more profound sense of body-awareness than the toddler has ever had before, it's relatively easy for her to grab any object at hand and attempt to decorate her own body with that object in some way, to see if the parent thinks it's funny. Things out of place, indeed!

Actions out of place will also make a parent smile or laugh. So, in order to liven up the dinnertime conversation, the toddler suddenly stands up in her chair and begins dancing at the dinner table. She gets away from the parent at bathtime and runs naked through the house— most parents will laugh at that, at least the first thirty times it happens. Perhaps a grandparent is there to appreciate the joke. Conceptual humor will arrive later, but for now the object-out-of-place or the action-out-of-place will work well for the toddler in terms of getting adults to laugh—and focusing the spotlight back on the toddler.

### Stress producer, stress reliever

How wonderful of God to have designed toddlers in such a way that they provide parents with the solution (well, at least a *partial* solution) to the dilemma of the toddler's own existence! All parents have the experience of feeling harried and stressed, and then suddenly laughing at their toddler's antics, alleviating at least part of the stress.

The extreme example of this is the toddler who suddenly pitches a full-blown fit, complete with headbanging on the floor and screams of agony—and what does the parent do? Burst out laughing! At the very moment when the parent might be experiencing the pains of having to deal with a recalcitrant toddler who is intent on running the universe her own way, there is something so funny about her actions that the parent can't help but laugh, and this laughter alleviates the very stress that might have been caused by the toddler's tantrum in the first place. So the toddler is both the dilemma and the solution at the same time.

Are there other situations in life where God has provided the problem and the answer at the same time? They are everywhere around us. We have only to look for the laughter in most of life's little quandaries in order to experience the grace of God's sense of humor. The wise believer, and the wise parent of a toddler, will look at life with an eye to seeing humor everywhere, allowing God's built-in solution to do what it does best— bring us back to a sense of the joy inherent in a relationship with the Author of love and humor. As you live with your toddler, keep laughing. Remember, "don't sweat the small stuff," but the big gift of humor can come wrapped in a small, toddler-sized package.

# Chapter 3

# Up, Up, and Away:
## Eighteen to Twenty-One Months

Your toddler is now one and a half years old. You cannot recall a time when you didn't have this delightful bundle of energy around. You also cannot recall a time when you sat down to read a book without worrying about doing the laundry at the same time, or when you could wait until 8:30 P.M. for dinner if you felt like it, or when you might have stayed in bed until noon just because you wanted to. The majority of your daily routine is dictated by the presence of your (mostly) cheerful two-foot-tall barrel of enthusiasm on legs. You are exhausted much of the time. And yet there are those moments of grace that mark the lives of toddlers in this age group. You can occasionally see the person your child will become. It is an exciting time to be a parent.

# Large Motor Skills: Altitude Is Best!

The eighteen to twenty-one month old delights in his own physical prowess and in his ability to demonstrate that prowess to you at every turn. In particular, altitude becomes a concern for him—and therefore, for his parents as well.

The eighteen month old is suddenly aware of, and fascinated with, the idea of *height*. He realizes that Mom and Dad are much taller than he is, and that the only way to get to that height is to convince them to pick him up. Or *is* it the only way to get to that height? . . . No! Suddenly, he figures out that he could climb onto things and perhaps reach, if not the height of the parents, at least a much higher plane than he has previously known on his own steam. So he goes about the house climbing on everything.

> **The eighteen month old is suddenly aware of the idea of *height*.**

***Climb every mountain (or sofa, or bookcase, or table . . .)***
The arms and legs now begin to work in a more coordinated fashion in order for him to pull himself onto counters, dressers, furniture, or porch railings. In fact, while the arms are *pulling* the upper body toward the object he grasps, the legs are *pushing* the lower body upward, away from the object on which he stands.

This combination of pulling and pushing requires a new kind of coordination at "brain central" in the central nervous system—two extremities, engaged in two slightly different activities, both for the purpose of moving the body upward against gravity. Add to this the fact that the left arm may be called on to do a slightly different action or grasp a slightly different object than the right arm, and the right leg may be pushing against something different than the left leg is pushing against (for example, the cushions of the sofa with one leg and the arm of the sofa with the other leg), and you have a truly remarkable feat! The brain coordinates all of this frenzied activity so that the body may be propelled upward at a great rate of speed.

So climbing becomes a key activity for the eighteen month old. This activity, and its inherent dangers for the toddler, is one of the reasons that the parents of toddlers are so exhausted and ready to sleep at a moment's notice. The average toddler-parent probably makes five life-saving catches per hour of time spent with the toddler, every day for several months. No major league baseball player can claim more impressive activity than that.

### Upstairs, downstairs

The toddler is getting better at climbing up—and *down*—stairs at this stage of life. Again, climbing up and climbing down both require different activities of arms and legs at this point. Either the arms are holding onto a handrail and pulling the child's body upward by grasping the handrail and pulling against gravity, or the arm/hand is being held by an adult as the child ascends the staircase. The adult holding a child's hand will usually stand alongside the child on a given step of the staircase, thereby steadying the child's arm/hand, but not allowing the arm to exert much (if any) pull against gravity.

After a few tries, the child will know this and may resist the attempts by the adult to help him up the staircase at home or up the steps of the playground slide. The toddler knows he can accomplish the physical work of climbing the stairs more efficiently if he is allowed to hold the handrail, and he will usually insist on that after his first few trips up the stairs.

Meanwhile, the legs are busy propelling the child upward by virtue of pushing the body away from the previous step. By placing a foot on the next step up and then rearranging his balance so that his weight is now shifted onto the new (higher) step, the child manages to climb the staircase. If the adult insists on helping the toddler climb the stairs, there may be a tantrum or a battle-of-wills, because the toddler understands that he actually accomplishes the mechanical work of climbing better without help from the parent, once the trick of shifting the body weight onto the upper foot is learned.

### God is ready to catch us

As you repeatedly catch your toddler falling from the heights today, remember this: God is also gracious about allowing us to use the muscles we have (or think we have) in order to climb in our own style. God's love never beats us over the head with our inadequacies or failures, nor does it insist we climb in the way that might be easiest for us. We are free to make our own moves and our own mistakes. We are allowed the freedom to climb, to fall backwards, to scoop ourselves up and try again. We are surrounded and supported by

Eternal Love as we advance on our spiritual journey.

> **God's love never beats us over the head with our own inadequacies or failures.**

What a wonderful model for parenting our toddlers (or for that matter, our teenagers!). Love that supports, and never diminishes, the efforts of the loved one is a profound gift. Consider how you are reflecting that love the next time you see a toddler busily climbing the staircase in order to reach new heights.

## Small Motor Skills: Even Picasso Had to Begin Somewhere

The eighteen to twenty-one month old now uses his hands with abandon, rarely exhibiting the fascination with them that he showed at four months, nine months, or even a year of age. He now understands that his hands are extensions of his arms, and therefore, of himself. They are there to do his bidding, and to do it with a minimum of fuss. The problem is he doesn't have the fine motor skills yet to move his fingers in exactly the ways he desires. Sometimes he approaches the learning of small, fine motor skills with ease and confidence. Other times, he approaches fine motor tuning with fear and trepidation, or with frustration inherent in each movement. Assuring him that even great artists had to begin by learning how to hold a pencil is little comfort to the toddler at this stage.

### Slight of hand

As your child grows, both arms and legs have to be "cemented" into the central nervous system by the maturing of the nerves along that extremity. This process is called *myelination,* as a coating of myelin, a wonderful protein substance that enhances electrical signals along the length of neurons, is laid down on the outside of each neuron. This myelination allows signals to be sent from brain to muscle and back to brain in a fraction of a second.

The entire maturation process happens for the arms first, then the legs. The fine-tuning of that process occurs more acutely for the arms and hands than it does for the legs and feet. Although some of us retain the ability to pick objects up with our feet, most of us are much better at it using our hands. Certainly Mozart, who could play the keyboard upside down and backwards, never played the harpsichord very well with his feet! We also know that the process works from the proximal part of the extremity (closer to the brain) to the distal part (further from the brain). So the fine-tuning of the hands and the use of individual fingers in a coordinated fashion is the last motor skill to be honed in the young human.

> **The use of individual fingers is the last motor skill to be honed in the young human.**

## *Sign here, please*

The eighteen- to twenty-one-month-old toddler, of course, is completely unaware of all this physiology. He only knows that he can grasp a pencil or a crayon in his fist and scribble on paper with it as he sees his parents do. The cause-and-effect of making the mark on paper delights him and is completely consistent with his idea that he runs the universe. The toddler will grasp the marking instrument in whatever fashion he can, make the mark (on whatever he can), and feel a sense of supremacy and pride. The fine points of how to curl the fingers around the pencil, or even which side of the fist the pencil lead is on, are details he will pay attention to later. For now, it is enough to make his impression.

The toddler at this age will attempt many other hand skills as well. He will hold a block in his hands, turning it over and over. He will attempt to throw many objects around the house (the inflatable ninety-nine-cent beach balls are good for throwing in the house). He will be fascinated with the remote control for the TV or stereo system, and in the process of learning how to push just *one* button on the device, he will develop more finely-honed abilities to stab an object with just *one* finger. He will be able to use a fork and a spoon for purposes of feeding himself and be fairly accurate at getting food onto the utensil and then the utensil into his mouth—with soup being the treacherous exception there. All of these skills utilize as much wrist movement as they do finger motion. The wrist movements must be learned before we graduate to fine movements of the fingers.

## One thing at a time

As we watch the eighteen to twenty-one month old move his wrists around and jab at objects with his fingers, we are reminded that we, too, move through spiritual growth in stages. The apostle Paul talked about walking and then running, about the normal course of human development, and about "seeing and doing things as a child" and then giving up childish things as he matured. He even chastised some Christians because he felt they were not growing up and were remaining "fat babies" in the faith (the Amy Grant song puts it well).

One point we can learn from toddler development: we *can* accomplish things at each stage of development and enjoy our accomplishment. The eighteen- to twenty-one-month-old toddler feels no shame that he cannot play Tchaikovsky's First Violin Concerto. He merely rejoices in his skill of being able to make a mark on a piece of paper using the muscles of the wrist. He does what his body allows him to do and pushes his skill level along as he tries new things. He does not regret his inabilities but takes joy in his abilities.

> **He does not regret his inabilities but takes joy in his abilities.**

Do we adults allow ourselves the same joy? Do we marvel at what God can do, and is doing, in us at each step along the way? Or do we secretly envision how "wonderful" we might be as Christians someday and only focus our vision of ourselves on that "someday believer"? Do we rob ourselves of the joy of discovery, the joy of learning new things in the spiritual realm, because we feel guilty that we can't do it better? What a waste of time and energy! How wise of the eighteen-month-old toddler to take at face value what he can do and what he can't do yet—and how much we may need that lesson in our own lives of faith!

Our God is a God of process, not just finished works. We have the right, as children of the Light, to fail, to question, to wonder, knowing that the God of grace is patient and faithful as we learn to follow his ways. We can express all the emotions we have rather than "hold in" our feelings as we stand before our Creator. Paul reminds us in Philippians that the God "who began a good work in you will carry it on to completion" (1:6). If that doesn't describe a God who rejoices in *process,* I don't know of any words that could. If God can love us "in process," surely we can learn to love ourselves in process too. If you can't remember what that looks like, watch an eighteen month old scribble on paper, and rejoice in the God who loves us for all time, in all things.

## Social Skills: The Toddler Creed Emerges

The eighteen- to twenty-one-month-old toddler has been the center of his own universe for quite some time, and probably the center of his parents' world as well. Suddenly, he emerges as a creature who seeks social interaction—occasionally, casually, and on his own terms, of course, but he seeks that interaction nonetheless.

The child this age has been interacting with adults for all of his life. He smiles at them, talks with them. He has wanted them to carry him, support him as he walks his first steps, roll a ball to him, play peekaboo and "so big," or practice waving bye-bye with him. Adults are natural to interact with, because they are caretakers for the infant-now-toddler. But suddenly, whether through a playgroup, a Sunday school class, or just casually at the playground, he has the opportunity to interact with *other humans his own age.* And this takes skills that he has never learned before, some of which take years of practice to master. (I can think of several adults I've met who have yet to master those skills.)

### *Mine!*

The eighteen to twenty-one month old first develops interaction with other toddlers around the issue of *ownership*—that is, who owns or commands a toy, a tricycle, a slide, a toy truck or car. One toddler is playing happily with the ball, and the next minute another toddler has picked it up and walked off with it. This violates the first toddler's sense that he owns the object, or at least commands its attention, and so he rushes to take the ball back, or to push the other toddler in frustration and rage. (Sounds like some politics, doesn't it?) A fight ensues, which will end in both toddlers screaming and crying, perhaps having done each other some physical damage in the interaction. Issues of biting, scratching, and hitting first emerge at this stage of a child's development. And it's all about ownership of *objects* (or, as the political scientists would say it, *resources*). It is no accident that the child's first pronoun is "mine"—it reflects his view of the entire world.

In fact, the "Toddler Creed" is in full force during this stage of human interaction. Some clever person— probably the parent of a toddler—came up with a list of basic rules toddlers live by. For those who have not seen it, the Toddler Creed goes like this:

1. If I want it, it's mine.
2. If I give it to you and change my mind later, it's mine.
3. If I can take it away from you, it's mine.
4. If I had it a little while ago, it's mine.
5. If it's mine, it will never belong to anyone else, no matter what.
6. If we are building something together, all the pieces are mine.
7. If it looks like mine, or like one I have ever had, it's mine.

You can see right away that two eighteen- to twenty-one-month-old toddlers each operating under this system of universal justice-according-to-self will run into big problems negotiating the fine points of who owns (or controls) what. And this quality interaction will suddenly cause new headaches for the parent(s) of the child.

> **Issues of biting, scratching, and hitting first emerge at this stage.**

### Playtime dilemma

Up until now, your toddler has had interactions primarily with you or with your friends and family. Perhaps an older sibling or cousin has interacted with the child briefly under controlled—we hope—circumstances. But now, for the first time, the parents are asked to mediate a relationship, however tenuous, between their child and another child of the same age, who does *not* have the sensitivity or sensibility of an adult. Both toddlers are, if you will, out for blood, and they don't care who gets trampled along the way as long as they get their own wish, their own needs attended to, and they remain the parents' top priority.

This creates a new dilemma for the parents. How do you make two toddlers happy at the same time, when their wishes diverge exactly 180 degrees from each other? "Do I convince my child to subvert his wishes to the desires of the other child? Do I attempt to work out a compromise? Does my child always have to be the one to 'give in'?" These and a hundred other variations on the question arise in the blink of an eye for most parents.

The simple answer, and one that works in most situations quickly, is to stress the value of sharing. It is usually possible with toddlers for adults to work out a quick and easy compromise: "You play with this toy for five minutes, and I'll find something new and interesting for the other child, and then after five minutes, we'll switch." The fact of the matter is, the attention from the adult usually solves the dilemma in the first place, and most toddlers have forgotten five minutes later that there was a conflict or a "deal" struck at all.

But this is a major developmental step in the life of

the toddler, and therefore in the life of the parents as well. The toddler begins to relate to others his own age, others who have nothing invested in keeping this toddler happy or in giving this toddler all the attention and spotlight, others who have no better large motor, small motor, language, or social skills than the toddler himself! It is a sobering thought, but one that every parent of a toddler faces.

### Grown up?

Does the Toddler Creed remind you of anyone you know who is *not* a toddler? If you're feeling brave right now as you read this, go find a mirror and look into it for a full sixty seconds (yes, time it!). Every one of us acts out the Toddler Creed now and again, some of us on a very regular basis. Perhaps it's not always with an object. Perhaps it's with *time,* or attention, or conversation (or lack thereof). Whatever the medium, the fact is that we all act on our own whims, our own desires more often than we might like to acknowledge. We all wish to be the center of attention, the center of someone's loving actions, most of the time. We *all* wish to own the control, the resources, at every possible turn. That is the human condition.

> **Every one of us acts out the Toddler Creed now and again.**

We cannot escape that kind of egocentrism, not even by cloaking it in "doing good for others" or some other clever cover-up. It is who we are and how we live. And God, with infinite love and mercy, loves us anyway. The next time you are forced to mediate a relationship between two toddlers, recall that God mediates relationships among six billion of us, all at the same time. That thought makes creating oceans and mountains, stars and galaxies, kind of small potatoes, doesn't it? And God loves us with perfect love, with perfect grace, with perfect patience. What a gift of remembrance your toddler's interpersonal squabbles can be!

# Language Skills: "I Seem to Be a Verb"

Buckminster Fuller, the inventor of the geodesic dome and hundreds of other things, wrote a book entitled *I Seem to Be a Verb*. This phrase epitomizes both the energy level of the eighteen- to twenty-one-month-old toddler and the language issues he deals with at the moment. The eighteen to twenty-one month old has probably got a vocabulary of twenty-five to two hundred words. He is adding nouns to his list of usable words all the time, and probably has a few pronouns to use as well. This allows the formation of two-word phrases such as "up, Daddy" and "kitty under" (the chair). These phrases capture his knowledge of the objects in the world around him and give the sense that he can *order* the world of objects, at least by expressing the relationship of those two objects to each other.

### Eat, run, walk
But now the toddler begins to notice and imitate the

sounds of *verbs* in the language he is learning. The nouns can *do* things and can have actions or be acted upon. So the dog, which the toddler has known from birth, is now identified by name and also *jumps* or *eats* or *runs*. The toddler is beginning to notice his own actions in the world and to categorize those actions. He himself runs, or jumps, or eats, or dances. He carries the ball, or throws it—but he doesn't eat the ball. He eats crackers, or apples, or grapes—but he doesn't (in the best of all possible worlds) throw them. By categorizing and identifying actions, he begins to establish a sense of social propriety in the world, and in order to identify and categorize those actions, he needs a discrete word for each action. So he begins to clue in to the use of verbs by adults and others around him.

He will imitate verb usage quite readily, as long as adults use a single verb to identify a single action—synonyms are strictly forbidden in toddler-ese (they will come later). So the toddler will use the word *jump* and then *do* the action of jumping. If he gets a nod and a verbal response from an attentive adult, he may try to repeat the action several dozen times, until well after the adult tires of the game. But this is how he learns the meaning of the verb *jump*. He will try similar means to learn the definitions of another one hundred verbs or so in the next year. This progression of noun-to-preposition-to-pronoun-to-verb seems to be universal among all language groups in all cultures of the world. (For a wonderful discussion of how the human brain is wired for language acquisition, see Steven Pinker's book *The Language Instinct.*)

> # The toddler will start to imitate verb usage quite readily.

### *Toddler words of wisdom*

A toddler's language-acquisition skills provide an analogy to our spiritual lives. We first learn about God's love and grace in our lives and about how that love supports us in all things. As we grow spiritually and understand more fully what it is to "walk the talk" of the Christian life, we develop an appreciation of the "verbs" of the faith—the actions. We learn about praying, giving, and developing our talents and gifts. We learn about forgiving ourselves and others. We learn about turning over the details of our existence to the Author of all action, of all love. And we come to realize that *love* is not a noun, but a verb, a way of life. How kind of the eighteen- to twenty-one-month-old toddler to remind us of the essential things in our lives—to remind us that the ultimate action, the ultimate victory, is to love in all circumstances and situations. What a "good word" every toddler speaks!

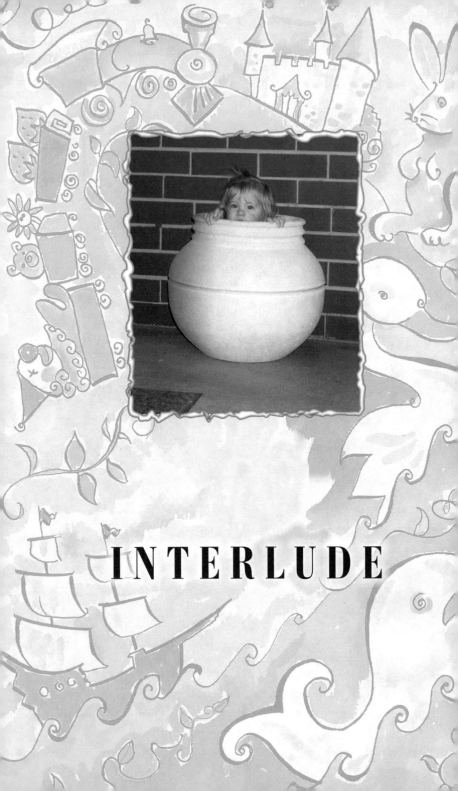

# INTERLUDE

# The Toddler and Change

*God is over all things,*
*under all things,*
*outside all,*
*within, but not enclosed,*
*without, but not excluded,*
*above, but not raised up,*
*below, but not depressed,*
*wholly above, presiding,*
*wholly without, embracing,*
*wholly within, filling.*
—*Hildevert of Lavardin, eleventh-century writer*

Anyone who has lived with toddlers knows that they don't deal with change easily. Take a normal eighteen month old who sleeps through the night to Grandma's house for a week, where he must sleep in an unfamiliar place, and you will certainly have two weeks' worth of wakeful nights upon your return home. I tell the parents of toddlers to keep, if possible (and, granted, it's not always possible!), the same living space they have until after the child is two years old—your lives will go more easily because of this. Any time you change a toddler's routine for even a *short* period of time (i.e., two days), you are likely to invoke tantrums and whiney, clingy behavior for several days or weeks.

Why does the toddler seem to resist change so adamantly? I believe that the answer lies at the crossroads between two distinct, but related concepts. The first concept is that the toddler runs the universe and everything should go according to *his* plan. The second concept, and one that explains *much* of a toddler's behavior, is the confusion of *predictability* with *causation.* The toddler mistakenly thinks that if he can *predict* something, then he *caused* it to occur. When he comes tearing around the corner into the living room, he always glances at the sofa to see where it is. If it is in the same place day after day, he quickly comes to believe that he *made* the sofa to exist on that wall, and all is well.

If, on the other hand, he lives with parents who enjoy rearranging the furniture often, he will come around the corner into the living room some day soon and see that the sofa is on a *different* wall than he imagined or predicted. This fact runs completely counter to his notion of running the universe, and he will therefore plunge himself onto the floor, wailing. Or he may just exhibit the typical toddler "bad day" phenomena of clinging, crying often, and wanting *lots* of attention from parents. I suggest to parents that they make an attempt to keep as much the same in the toddler's environment as possible during the fifteen- to twenty-four-month time period, to lighten their own load a bit and keep their toddler on an even keel.

A gentle warning for parents: As you can tell, eighteen months is probably not the ideal spacing between children, precisely because of this inability to cope with change on the part of your first-born. The problem is, six month olds are so cute and cuddly, so entertaining, that many parents think "this is such a wonderful adventure—let's do it again!" Then, nine to twelve months later, they have on their hands a raging toddler who *used* to be a cute and cuddly infant, along with a newborn to care for. Both are handfuls all by themselves. Put them together and you have an exhausted set of parents. Just a warning!

### A *mighty fortress*

How interesting that toddlers should be programmed to need things to *be the same* at this stage of their lives, especially since they were created by a God who seems to love, thrive on, and create change both on a universal level and in the lives of human beings. Perhaps the toddler's need for predictability is genetically programmed into humans at such an early age to illustrate that, by contrast, the *adult* way of approaching life is to expect change. Maturity somehow equals the ability to "roll with the punches" and accept change at all times, in all places. Perhaps the ultimate message here is that God is our unchanging rock, and that although everything else (and I mean *every*thing else) in our lives can change, the love of God is still there for us, unfailing and unchangeable. The toddler's inability to cope with change can be a reminder of God's promise to never leave us. It is a reminder that we are carved on the palm of God's hand (Isaiah 49:16), and no matter what the changes are in our lives, God is the immutable constant.

# Chapter 4
# All the World's a Stage:
## Twenty-One to Twenty-Four Months

Your toddler is now able to motor around the house at top speed. She is able to communicate her wants without crying (maybe). She will sit on a lap to listen to a story for several minutes-to-hours, although *she* wants to be the one to decide which book gets read. You, as the parent of this marvel, are beginning to get the rhythm of change into your bloodstream. You begin to understand in new ways how awesome the task of parenting will be for the next twenty years. In other words, you're getting "broken in." What can you expect from your twenty-one to twenty-four month old as you approach the "terrific twos?"

# Large Motor Skills: In the Spotlight

The twenty-one- to twenty-four-month-old person is ever-better at climbing, at jumping, at eluding the parents' grasp in all kinds of situations. The arms and the legs work together in ever-improved ways. It has been said of this toddler that she "thinks with her feet," running around until she literally bumps into an object and then exploring the object she has met. She may poke, prod, or thrust other objects at the object that was in her way on her circuit of the house. The toddler now uses large motor skills to solve problems without whining or asking the parent for help.

### *Jump!*

One particular skill that the twenty-one to twenty-four month old may develop is the standing broad jump. An adult will accomplish this motion with much swinging of the arms in order to use the momentum of the arms to gain distance on the jump. A toddler will not (necessarily) use the arms to gain momentum—that is more sophisticated stuff and requires more balance than the toddler has just now. (If you see a toddler using the arms effectively in the standing broad jump, please contact the U.S. Olympic track team coach as soon as possible!)

An adult will rock forward onto the ball of the foot and then backwards onto the heel as part of the momentum build-up activity from the standing position to the jump itself. The toddler merely tightens the quadriceps muscle of the upper thigh in order to bend the knee slightly. By giving a little pushoff with the ball of the foot and then bending the knees, the toddler manages to get both feet off the ground at the same time, thus giving "a jump."

### Look at me!

The twenty-one to twenty-four month old will not be content to have the skill and know she has done a good job, she will also take every opportunity to show off this skill in a social context. Many times a day parents and caregivers will hear the words (however babbled), "Hey, look! Watch this!" and then be called on to admire yet one more broad jump. In fact, seeking the limelight is a characteristic of this age and is approached as an entirely new activity with each new skill acquired.

This need to show off a skill actually becomes part of the skill itself, rather than just a natural consequence of the skill. The twenty-one month old sees new ways of moving her body as *a part of herself* at this age. Asking a parent to admire the new skill is only another way to say "play with me" or "interact with me."

> **This need to show off a skill becomes part of the skill itself.**

The toddler is more aware of a large motor (move-your-entire-body) skill she has acquired than she is aware of other acquired skills, and so these are the ones she chooses to show off. Few toddlers will demonstrate their ability to balance blocks or solve a stacking-toy puzzle with as much enthusiasm as they demonstrate their ability to jump or climb. Moving the entire body at this stage constitutes a *major,* and therefore laudable, skill. Only later will it dawn on the child that moving the fingers in order to play the piano or place delicate jigsaw puzzle pieces together might also be a skill worthy of note by adults. For now, the toddler moves *all* of herself and congratulates herself on her cleverness, expecting any adult to do the same.

### Glory to God

Do we sometimes "show off" on our journey as believers? Do we have the need to be the center of the spotlight in the church, in our workplace, in our home life? Do we call attention to ourselves, and our work, in order to hear that "good job" commendation from others? Jesus talked about doing good deeds in secret, not for the rewards of human beings but for the sheer sake of doing a good thing. He specifically told his followers *not* to pray loudly in the temple so that others would hear the prayers, but to go to a quiet place and pray, so that only God would know (Matthew 6:5-6). God made us to be in relationships and to appreciate encouragement, but if we constantly look for the approval of others, we will be disappointed. When we seek first the approval of *God,* we act out of right motivations and humble desires.

At times we want to steal the limelight even from God. We congratulate ourselves on some spiritual milestone and forget it is only by God's grace that we grow. It may be easy to see that our toddler wants to be the center of attention to show off a new motor skill, but we might also ask ourselves, "Where does that need to be center stage come from in *my* life? Am I acting for my own glory or for the glory of God?" For some, giving up the spotlight is the hardest sacrifice of all, but it is a necessary offering on the way to becoming like Christ. The place where we have laid our spotlight-need may be the precise place where our true journey with God can begin.

> **At times we want to steal the limelight even from God.**

# Small Motor Skills: Life with a Flourish

A toddler this age not only can motor her body around in new—and socially compelling—ways, but she can begin to do visual *art*. All her life she has seen adults with pen and paper in hand. Dad makes a list for the grocery store and then crosses things off as he fills the cart. Mom takes notes on a newspaper article or writes out a check. Grandma may write a note to someone on a nice notecard. The caregiver at the church nursery takes notes on what she or he is told about a particular child. All around her, the toddler has seen people wielding pens, pencils, paper. And suddenly, she has the motor skills necessary to grasp the pencil, *and* the interest to begin to scribble or draw or "write."

The child generally grasps the pen first with all four fingers wrapped around the stem of the writing instrument. The thumb may be placed on the opposite side from the fingers (i.e., so that thumb meets fingertips), or it may wrap around the same side as the fingers. Whichever way it goes, the child attempts to mark on the paper with a pen or pencil with the writing end protruding from either side of the hand (that is, the writing tip may be nearest the little finger or it may be nearest the thumb). After the child understands that the mark may be made with the writing instrument, that instrument will probably become a source of fascination for the child. Toddlers can often be distracted by a pen and paper. The twenty-one month old understands that this is important to try because adults everywhere seem to be doing it.

The child may then begin to experiment with different hand positions around the pen. Is it more comfortable to write with the thumbside down, next to the paper, or with the thumb away from the paper? Generally, only a few tries will convince her that thumbside *up* is more comfortable. This is because the pronating muscles of the forearm are in a more "at rest" position when the thumb is up—try it yourself! Does it feel better to have the thumb encircling the stem of the pen, or aligned with the fingers on one side of the stem? Again, the position of muscles "at rest" will determine what feels most comfortable with any given position.

### Art studio

Once the child has figured out which position feels best for holding the pen, she begins to experiment with scribbles on paper. Do large diagonal slashes look better than groupings of short strokes all going the same direction? What happens when you hold the pen to paper continually for several different directions? How dense can a scribble be? Do holes in the paper, created by the pen point, enhance the look?

And what happens when you can add *color* to your

artwork? If green goes one direction and red another on the paper, does it look good? Will blue go over yellow and still look blue? How does orange crayon on orange construction paper look? Your child is learning a myriad of things about the visual world around her, while at the same time practicing fine motor skills with the hands. This kind of crossover learning between skill groups will continue for all of her life. (Educators call it *integrated learning situations.*)

> **Toddlers can often be distracted by a pen and paper.**

### Timber!

Meanwhile, the twenty-one to twenty-four month old is building with blocks, a fine-motor skill of another sort. The ability to make a tower of blocks involves motor movements of the arm as well as of the hand and fingers. One must be able to get enough of block 2 to follow the silhouette of block 1 (the base block, the one sitting on the floor) to keep the creation's center of gravity inside the edges of block 1. If one then wishes to stack a third block on top of 1 and 2, block 3 must also match the silhouette of 1 and 2 enough to keep the center of gravity of all *three* blocks aligned within the edges of block 1.

This, for the builder, involves movement of the shoulder, the upper arm, the forearm, and the muscles of the hand that is grasping the blocks. In addition, the hand must not accidently brush blocks 1 and 2 in placing 3, or the whole mess will tumble. So stacking a group of blocks is really quite a sophisticated exercise in three-dimensional reality. At first, your toddler will be able to stack two, then three blocks. By age two, she may be able to stack four in succession. More than four blocks stacked will usually fall.

### *Just my style*

It's probably a good idea to mention once again how the child's learning style plays a role in what she's *capable* of doing and what she's *interested* in doing—which can be two entirely separate things:

The child with a *visual* learning style will be interested in looking at the world. As infants, these children were often happy to sit for long periods of time looking at the world around them from their infant seats and "taking mental notes." When they needed a change of pace, carrying them to a new place to see something new—perhaps a picture on a wall, a mirror—would suffice. These children are usually interested in such things as artwork, picture puzzles, and books.

The child with an *auditory* learning style will be very attuned to sounds. You may have noticed that as an infant this child's mood could be entirely turned around through the use of music. If she began to fuss, playing soft, soothing music made her a new person. These children often hum to themselves while playing, or even while nursing as very young infants. They are quick to pick up on the difference between sounds and can usually replicate sounds made by parents quickly and easily. They also replicate the accents necessary to speak another language more quickly and more accurately than their visual or kinesthetic colleagues.

The *kinesthetic* child is the kid who is always moving. Usually, especially in the early months and years of life, this movement involves the whole body rather than just an arm or a leg. These are the children who walk early, crawl ahead of time, "are into everything" at a young age. These folks are not the snuggly babies; they may desire comfort for a moment, but then they need to be down on the floor so that they can *move.* These are the tough kids who fall, brush themselves off, and move on to the next physical task at hand, rather than wailing and needing comfort from a parent.

These are the three basic learning styles for which the human brain appears to be "wired." Of course, most of us learn through a combination of the different styles. Most kinesthetic learners also process information visually or auditorially, for instance. But the parent of the twenty-one- to twenty-four-month-old toddler will do well to keep in mind that a child's learning style will influence what she learns as well as how she learns.

> **Most of us learn through a combination of the different styles.**

Watch how your toddler approaches the large and small motor skills at this stage, and you will know much about how she will approach life in the future. Is she happy to play on the floor with a stacking toy and with toys that need manipulation with the hands? Or is she happiest when she can move her entire body, running, jumping, climbing, and swinging? Does she spontaneously sing? Or does she prefer to dance without singing? Does she enjoy going through books to point out objects on each page, or does she prefer to hear the story from beginning to end without interruption? All of these observations will tell you something about how your toddler processes information, as well as *what* information she will be interested in processing. An awareness of learning style will help the savvy parent in many situations in the months and years ahead.

### Same God, diverse creation

Why did God create human beings with so many different learning styles? Why aren't we all just the same, with the same capabilities to notice things in the environment, the same cultural answers to the questions of survival, the same in our perceptions of and beliefs about the God who created us all?

The geneticist would answer, "Because minor genetic variations dictate that genetically determined characteristics will be different in different members of the same species." The anthropologist might answer, "Because there is a selective advantage to the group that has members who can see (or hear, or manipulate objects in space) better than members of another group/species. All three capabilities *together* represented in the group would allow that group to better answer the questions of survival in any given environment."

But the Christian theologian would answer, "Because God is a God who celebrates diversity and delights in each individual as a unique creation." And the pastor or spiritual director would answer, "God created people with many different learning styles so that all would have to work together, and each would have to learn to rely on the strengths of another person in the work of the kingdom of God here on earth." So as you watch your toddler learn small motor skills, remember that she is teaching you to celebrate the diversity of God's creation.

Growing toddlers can also remind us that we each have our own unique *spiritual* learning style. We all grow closer to God through a variety of means. We may recognize divine truth, however, more clearly in certain ways than in others. In what ways do you most vividly relate to God? Through nature? Hearing Scripture read aloud? Moving to music? Contemplative prayer? Consider your style of spiritual learning and how you can learn from the styles of other people you know. Enjoy how God uses our diversity to unify us and bring us closer to Love's unchanging character.

## Social Skills: "Yours" as well as "Mine"

New adaptive abilities are often seen in twenty-one to twenty-four month olds as they begin to move away from the unbridled egocentrism and self-absorption of the eighteen-month age. One of the most conspicuous— and delightful—changes of this age is an interest in and ability to distinguish ownership of objects. Many toddlers are now aware of what belongs to whom, and they will tell you so in no uncertain terms. Your toddler may suddenly begin to let you know who owns what in the family. While at eighteen months she cared only about what was "mine," now she can begin to care about what is "yours" too. Your toddler may suddenly say "Mommy's keys" or "baby's book." She may be aware of "Daddy's newspaper" or "the kitty's dish." (All of these awarenesses are in the context of home. At the store, a child this age may walk off with anything, assuming it is for her.)

> **Your toddler may suddenly begin to let you know who owns what in the family.**

The toddler at this stage may also have a good idea of where many household objects go and will actually enjoy putting things in their place (remember to bottle this capability and save it for the teenage years!). Toddlers often enjoy putting the folded laundry away, storing the (plastic) kitchenware, or stacking CDs and books in the appropriate place. They may enjoy unpacking after a trip or putting silverware away after the dishwasher finishes its job.

Child-development experts Ames and Ilg, in their book *Your One Year Old*, tell the story of a little girl this age who had a cracker in one hand and attempted to pick up a package of crayons with the other hand. She accidentally dropped one crayon out of the box. She then tried to put the package in the same hand with her cracker in order to pick up the dropped crayon. Failing, she tucked the crayon box between her forearm and body and then picked up the crayon from the floor. In other words, instead of merely looking for help, the twenty-one to twenty-four month old may often solve problems for herself. Someone attempting to be helpful with a toddler this age may receive an annoyed *no* from the child as she diligently tries to do it on her own.

### Can I play?

During these months the child may attempt to play with another child for the first time. The toddler's new awareness of other people's ownership of things allows the child to begin the mental negotiation necessary for cooperative play. If what you have is what I wish to play with, and if I can clearly identify that it is *yours* (if only by right of possession at the moment), then if I am going to play with that object, I had better figure out a way to play *with* you (ah, if only world geopolitical viewpoints were as clear!). While the cooperative play is unquestionably motivated by self-interest, at least the twenty-one-month-old toddler has a glimmer of how to get along with a playmate. Later, plots and miniplays will come into view as players take on roles (such as "Mommy" and "Daddy") on a stage. For now, the toddler is content—most of the time—to play with the same objects as a friend plays with, thereby defining the first steps in cooperative play.

Incidentally, since toddlers really don't play *with* other children until around this age, I often suggest that parents wait until that time to begin play groups, for their own peace of mind as well as because the groups just don't seem to do much for the children. I have found over the years that infant play groups and even toddler play groups do more to heighten a parent's anxiety than anything else. Most parents end up comparing their child to one child in the group regarding large motor skills, another child in the group regarding small motor skills, a third for language skills, and often a fourth for social skills. The end result? A parent who is convinced that his or her child will never be "good" at anything, or worse, a parent who is convinced that her child is "behind" the peer group. Of course, comparing notes with other parents of toddlers can be of benefit, and if that's why a parent chooses to do a play group, that decision may have merit. But the recent trend of engaging in play groups because one might be seen as a "bad" parent if one doesn't participate is *not,* in my mind, a good reason to participate!

### In community

And what does this first stage of cooperative play tell us about the nature of God? What can we glean from watching the twenty-one- to twenty-four-month-old toddler in the social setting? We can learn that God is apparently so intent on bringing humans to the throne of grace *as a community* that any means, no matter how self-centered, will be used to drag us along toward spiritual maturity.

> **Community yields many spiritual rewards that a life in isolation cannot afford us.**

Just as the toddler cannot look ahead to the teen years and realize that the day will come when the peer group is "everything" in her world, so we cannot always see ahead to comprehend the importance of the spiritual community. The beginning believer may not be able to appreciate how much we are pushed to growth by the presence of other believers in our life. Support, prayer, love, and help can all be offered by the spiritual community around us in ways that the rest of the world cannot help. The mature form of "cooperative play" yields many spiritual rewards that a life in isolation cannot afford us.

As you watch your twenty-one month old take those first tentative steps toward cooperative play with another child of similar age, remember that she is not motivated by the noblest of ideals but by the selfish wish to play with a desired object. In our own spiritual journey, are we motivated to a life in community by what that community can do for *us,* or by what we have to give to that community in the name of God's love and caring? Are we being God's hands and feet in the world around us out of self-centered motivations or because we try to emulate the Divine Model who came to earth to take on the form of a servant?

## Language/Communication Skills: Saying It More Clearly

Here I should mention that girls at this age may be well ahead of boys in speech skills, both in vocabulary and in fluency of speech. A twenty-one-month-old boy may be speaking chiefly in one or two word phrases, using primarily babbled jargon without much content, or he may even be continuing to point and say *eh-eh* as his primary means of communication. By contrast, a twenty-one-month-old girl may already be speaking in short sentences, even though the articulation may not be clear. In particular, consonant combinations ("pl," "tr," "sh," "th," and "cr") may not be pronounced. Most twenty-one to twenty-four month olds will enunciate one of those consonants but not the other. "Clear" may be "cear," "please" becomes "peas," "shoe" may be "soe." However, words with a consonant at both the beginning and the end of the word will probably be pronounced with some kind of consonant sound at both ends of the word. Thus, "train" becomes "tain," no longer "tay"; "cat" may be pronounced correctly; and the word for father may now be "Dad," not "Da."

Most twenty-one month olds enjoy practicing language opportunities at every occasion. The toddler asked to put a letter into her mother's hand may say "into, into, into," giving the letter over and over again to the mother. But it's also true that both boys and girls may be suddenly immobilized and stand rigid with frustration if they don't have the words they need to make their desires known. Then the parent may see the child turn to another activity, plead for attention in some other fashion, or throw a full-blown temper tantrum, as she attempts to deal with her language deficit.

> **Most twenty-one month olds enjoy practicing language opportunities at every occasion.**

## God's language

We get frustrated, too, when we can't communicate well. As you attempt to express to the world around you the love of God that has so profoundly changed your own life, be easy with yourself. Some days you will have all the words in place, some days you may have only a half-formed idea of what you want to say, and some days you may grapple to articulate your thoughts at all. Remember that just as you understand your toddler when she cannot express her entire thought process, God understands that we are not always able to communicate to others as we want to. Our task is to be willing. God will do the speaking through us if we open our lives and our hearts to the divine language of love.

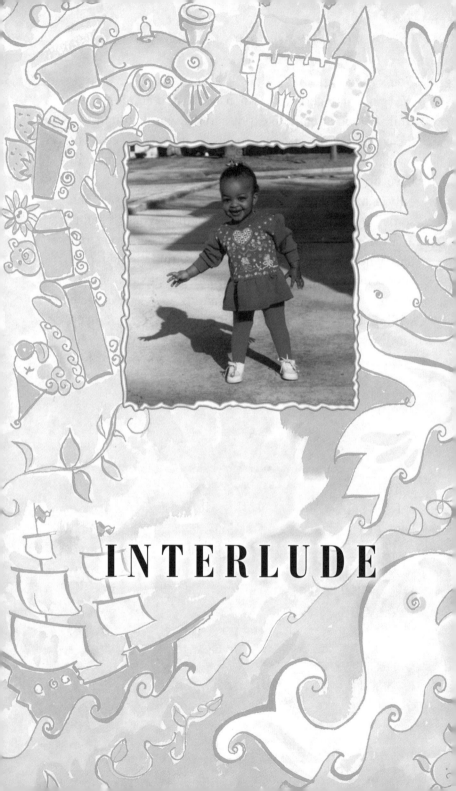

# INTERLUDE

# On Running the Universe

*No longer conscious of my movement, I*
*discovered a new unity with nature. I had found a*
*new source of power and beauty, a source*
*I never dreamt existed.*
—Roger Bannister, athlete, on breaking the 4-minute mile

The twenty-four-month-old child is full of herself—focusing on, and getting others to focus on, the feats that she can accomplish. She is able to command some attention in most settings. She can certainly let her opinion be known, whether in private with one parent, or in a fully public setting such as the grocery store or the shopping mall. And now she arrives at the conclusion that her opinion regarding any given activity or desired object carries more weight than anyone else's opinion—including that of a parent. The child becomes a victim of her own successes and carries the issue to the extreme, whatever the issue might be. How hard to live with. How arrogant. How incredibly human!

The two-year-old child assumes that she runs the universe, in large part because her view of the universe is very *small*. She makes the assumption that everyone's household runs on the same rules as hers does. She "knows" that other people live with the same furnishings, have a house with the same floorplan, drive the same car, read the same magazines, watch the same TV shows, and eat the same food as people do at her house. Therefore, if she understands (and rules) her own household, she will by extension be well-equipped to run every household in the neighborhood, in the city, in the state, in the country, in the hemisphere, on the planet (you get the idea).

One way to help a two year old with this "megalomania" is to explore the outside world with her. The wise parent will spend time pointing out that people drive different cars, live on different streets, eat different foods, wear varying styles of clothing. This may help the two year old expand her vision of the world and convince her that, while she's quite comfortable in the home setting, there could be many places that are new and strange to her—and of which she's not *quite* in control. The parent who verbalizes new observations and admits occasional surprise at a different circumstance is a wonderful model for the child. The child learns that new isn't necessarily *bad,* that people may differ in many ways and yet still be okay, and that it is perfectly acceptable to be surprised—even as an adult. She will "log" more of this information than any parent can possibly see at the moment.

By offering the child the gift of seeing the world as a bigger place than she has ever seen before, the parent is letting the child know that differences are to be expected whenever one encounters human beings. (While this is not a surprising thought to adults, it is certainly a shock to most two year olds.) Furthermore, it lets the child know that because there are always new and different encounters to be made, the child couldn't possibly control the whole world at once, all of the time.

Sometimes the two year old may rail against that thought—but sometimes she finds it a profound relief. By presenting the world as a positive place in which many details of living vary greatly among different groups of people, the child learns to explore the new while relying on the comfort and security of the old. The child gains confidence, both in her abilities as an explorer and a learner, and in the reliability of her family and household routines.

### Modeling normalcy

Many parents are concerned that they "need to be the same all the time" for their children to see them as sources of security. These parents berate themselves whenever they have a bad day, a screaming moment, or an hour of feeling totally overwhelmed. I try to remind parents that these times are, in fact, a tremendous *gift* to the child. It is very important for the child to see that normal human beings are, shall we say, uneven at best. After all, the child is a human also and will need to learn to cope with her own unevenness throughout her life. By modeling the fact that unevenness is normal, that in truth we were created with all of those emotions, and that emotions are not always logical, the parent is giving the child permission to be uneven herself.

Further, the parent is giving the child important clues as to how to find "evenness" after a time of unevenness.

Perhaps an old routine is soothing. Perhaps the parent needs to pound on the piano keys or on the workbench for a bit. Perhaps the parent needs to go for a run or play a game of tennis (modeling exercise and physical fitness for children is important, too!). Perhaps just a walk and a change of scenery will do it. All of these are options shown to the child, and so they all become possibilities for the child to emulate in the future.

Aware of their own feelings and willing to express those feelings rather than hide them, wise parents teach by example. Of course, *all* human beings at times think they run the universe—it is part of the human condition. And at times, we all rail against "not having our own way."

By allowing our children to appreciate the differences between people and by portraying those differences not as bad or suspect but as positive expressions of human individuality, we encourage them to appreciate the wonderful diversity of God's creation here on earth. We allow our children to see the world, and then the universe, for what it is: a constant dance, a celebration of the rhythms of God's creative power. We allow our children the respect they need to find their own way in the world, armed with the security of knowing God's infinite mercy and his joy in their very existence. We allow them to give over the running of *their* universe to the God of infinite power, infinite creativity, infinite love.

## Chapter 5
# Body in Motion:
## Twenty-Four to Thirty Months

The second year of life is a time dreaded by most parents. They look ahead to the "twos" as a time of enduring the unendurable. They quake with fear at the thought of keeping up with their toddler every second. They anticipate great battles for which they must "gird up their loins." They are right.

And yet, this can also be a time of great tenderness and sweetness on the part of the two year old. As I often tell parents, "when you've learned to negotiate the two-year-old battles, you are in prime shape for the teenage years." As the expression goes, it's sort of like trying to nail Jello to a tree—always slippery, often questioned as to "why-this-seemed-like-a-good-idea" when the adventure first began, and yet *very* instructive. This year reveals many things about who the child is, and also who the *parents* are (and what some of their own hidden motivations and unconscious needs might be) and how well the parents adapt to change. The flexibility parents learn now *will* help them be flexible when the child is a teenager; wise parents will rely on the same sense of adaptability for the teen years as they did for the toddler years. So, what are some of the characteristics of this age group? What does your toddler know now?

# Large Motor Skills: Ever-Larger Circles

The average two year old is much more confident in his motor abilities than he was a few short months ago. Now he can run, jump, climb, and hold objects with much more skill than he could previously. The world of movement is his. One way he expresses his pleasure in movement is to explore ways in which objects can help him move. Age two is the ideal time to try riding a tricycle if the trike is the right size for the child. The pleasure that the two year old feels in mastering a tricycle to make himself *go* is almost limitless.

> **The pleasure that the two year old feels in mastering a tricycle to make himself *go* is almost limitless.**

Pleasure is found in sitting not only on a tricycle but also on other straddle toys as well. This is the age when the rocking horse is popular. The "riding horse" that one still occasionally finds at supermarkets and shopping malls is *always* sought out. Two year olds will also straddle the bar on the swingset, pretending to ride a horse and *go*. Almost any toy that can be sat upon will be tried at this age, to experiment with the idea that the toy might enhance the toddler's mobility. It is an activity that allows control of his body, control of an object, and control of the world by being able to *move* in the world. Straddle toys offer all the best the world has to offer for the twenty-four to thirty month old.

### Enjoying the process

The early-two child seems to use his body more easily to obtain a goal, but he doesn't differentiate the goal from his method of *achieving* the goal. Activity is usually undirected, more for the sake of movement itself than because he wishes to get to a certain place. He climbs the monkey bars because he enjoys climbing, not because he specifically wishes to reach the top of the monkey bars. He fills a pail with sand, not because he wishes to have a pail of sand that he can move easily, but because he enjoys the activity of scooping sand with the shovel. He may climb onto a parent's lap, not because he truly wishes to be with the parent or to sit on the parent's lap for a story, but just because he wants to climb at that moment and a parent's lap is a safe place to climb. As soon as he is seated, he may begin his descent back to the floor, leaving the parent confused as to his initial intent. "Oh, you didn't *want* to read a story right now?!" may be the parent's conclusion. The answer is: No, of course not. The toddler merely wished to change altitude for a moment, in order to keep those climbing muscles warmed up.

### How to get there from here

You will notice, as your toddler makes his daily rounds to survey his kingdom, that he keeps the ankle and knee fairly rigid as he walks, creating the up-and-down bouncing gait of early two. This same lack of freedom in movement of the ankle is visible in how he propels the straddle toy. Watch carefully: he moves the tricycle by pressing down on the ground with his heels and pulling forward. The fact that his toes ever hit the ground is a mere by-product of his foot moving into the next forward position to plant the heels for the next pull.

You will also notice that the twenty-four to thirty month old tends to use both arms and legs *in pairs*—that is, they are doing the same movement at the same time. The more graceful alternate-arm-with-alternate-leg gait of the three year old will emerge later. For now, the both-legs-do-the-same-thing-at-the-same-time approach works very well for the straddle car and works well enough for him to ascend or descend stairs.

### Bending into God's love

Like toddlers in their walking style, adults have rigid points in their spiritual lives. We sometimes "lock" our spiritual knees or ankles, refusing to bend those places in order to accomplish the journey more easily. We latch on to one way of doing something, one way of praying, one method of focusing our attention or serving the kingdom, and we refuse to budge from that spot of comfort. We dig in our heels and steadfastly resist the vision of ourselves in a new task, a new venture, something outside our own zone of comfort.

Many times I have heard someone in a church say, "I'm not a public speaker. I could *never* get up and talk in front of a group." And yet, sometimes that is precisely what God calls us to do. At times in our lives God deliberately gives us an opportunity to try muscles we have never flexed, a chance to bend in a place we never saw as bendable before. There are times when the Spirit of God *pushes* us into an uncomfortable spot precisely so we can learn about the power of God's love working through us. We limit ourselves too often. We limit God's love too often. We forget that we are "created in the image of God," with the capability of learning new skills. We get too comfortable.

> **At times in our lives God gives us an opportunity to try muscles we have never flexed.**

As you watch your twenty-four to thirty month old motor around the patio or the playground on a straddle toy, remember that God may be pushing you to bend your knees and relax your ankles into a new place to stand. And remember that God's standards of "success" have nothing to do with the world's standards. God will love you whether you can make the Kiddie Kar go fast or slow—or whether (or not) you can make it go at all. God's love doesn't ask that we know how to do all the propelling of the vehicle, only that we be willing to sit down on the car and be open to *God* propelling the vehicle. Hang on for the ride of your life!

## Small Motor Skills: Getting It Together (and Taking It on the Road)

Large motor skills are not the only ones becoming more refined. Small motor skills are also progressing quite nicely in the twenty-four to thirty month old. The child can now put a simple puzzle together if the pieces are large enough. He enjoys paintbrushes, crayons, and pens, even if movements may still involve the entire arm rather than much flexion at the wrist. He can turn the pages of a book one by one; he can make a fist and then choose to wiggle his thumb, or move each finger separately (until thirty months, this usually happens while watching the fingers). Simple finger-games are a delight for this age group.

The twenty-four to thirty month old loves to take apart toys with big pieces and then put them back together again. He loves to string beads on a string, cut Play-Doh with a cookie cutter, unscrew jar lids, turn on faucets. In all of these activities, he is enjoying the activity of the hand as much as he is enjoying the effect that his hand has caused to happen. Some parents may get frustrated when the child forgets a task at hand because he is busy watching his hands do work. But the wise parent will expect this "losing the train of thought" and allow the toddler time and opportunity to study his hands and their abilities.

### On the move
At this age, certain things in the environment will be

constant reminders to try certain large motor and small motor skills. Every preschool teacher knows that a two year old cannot pass up a ladder or step without attempting to climb it. No twenty-four to thirty month old can resist the temptation to go up or down an inclined platform, and any hole in the wall or other aperture will be explored and poked with fingers or whole arms and hands. Movement catches the eye of the twenty-four to thirty month old as at no other time of life—he *must* chase the ball, he *must* run along behind the train, the tricycle, the wagon. Whereas the fifteen to eighteen month old enjoyed pulling a wagon or a toy on a string, the twenty-four month old wishes to *push* objects that roll. In this way, he makes the object move but can see the motion too. (Two year olds especially love to push their strollers or walkers around.)

> **The twenty-four month old wishes to *push* objects that roll.**

*People* in motion also prove irresistible to the two year old. He loves to chase a running child at the park, dance with a parent, walk alongside a known adult at church or in a shopping plaza. He loves to imitate the large motor movements of these people, but he is also willing to imitate their small motor movements. He will attempt to draw on the page after Mommy has drawn a picture of a cat. He will want to cut out biscuits from the dough himself after watching an adult do this. He will readily join in the building of blocks into a wall or a tower. He will be more than willing to build a sand-castle at the beach, particularly if an adult is already working on the project. He enjoys stacking and stirring. He is an adept imitator of movements large and small, although his true forte is replicating large motor movements.

### Developing individuality

While the eighteen month old worked the muscles of the hand together to accomplish a cooperative task that required all five fingers doing the same motion, the older twenty-four month old is willing to risk some *individuality* of the fingers for the sake of honing their skills. To get an idea of that individuality, look at your hands as you begin the finger-play "Here is the church and here is the steeple, open the doors and see all the people!" Fingers 3, 4, and 5 are doing the same motion (i.e., curled inside the fist and interlaced left and right), but the forefinger is extended at full stretch and pressed to the other forefinger, while the thumbs are adducted (pulled into the palm) and pressed together at their sides. That one position of the hands represents some of every motion that the human fingers can do. Considering that at each joint in the hand there are at least four sets of muscles, each capable of moving the fingers or parts of them in any one of four directions, to form the "church building" is a challenging set of directions for the twenty-four month old who is just learning to move individual parts of his hand.

We are often asked—more often than we recognize, I think—to risk some individuality within the church as well. God created each of us with unique gifts and talents. The apostle Paul tells us that each part of the body of Christ has its function, and that without the functioning of each individual part we cannot see the whole body function as it was designed to do (1 Corinthians 12). Yet so often we are afraid of expressing our individuality, of showing our gifts to the body of Christ.

> **God created each of us with unique gifts and talents.**

My guess is that many of us have even been programmed from early childhood not to *see* the unique gifts we have been given, perhaps so that we won't "make waves" or "stick out" in some way. But denying our God-given individuality creates a loss for the kingdom of God here on earth. Who will "step up to the plate" if we deny the gifts that we have? Who else may have the gift of hospitality in just the way that you do? Who may be able to write poetry with just your flair? Who may type up announcements, or bulletins, or book reviews for the church library if the one who has that gift fails to share it?

As you watch your twenty-four to thirty month old play "Here is the church . . . ," recall that each of the "people" inside that finger-church has a unique, and irreplaceable, fingerprint with which to make an imprint on the world. Your toddler is busy teaching his fingers to act independently of each other, which takes a certain kind of courage. Do we, as adults in the church, exhibit the same kind of courage? Will we respond to God's call to be who *we* were created to be?

## Social Skills: Acting It Out

The two year old has to learn about the entire world, and so touch and taste are utilized to explore all things around him. Any object that catches his attention, or for that matter almost anything at all, he explores with his hands. Most contact is brief, either with objects or with people. Since attention span is short, distractibility high, and inhibitions almost nonexistent, the twenty-four to thirty month old is attracted by many things, but few hold his attention or interest for long. Painting may keep his attention for a short period (three to five minutes), but the picture has little or no structure, and he will soon leave the painting for another activity. Once again, the *action* is more important than the actual product. Making large, sloppy strokes across paper with the paintbrush is more interesting than any picture that might be produced.

> **Attention span is short, distractibility high, and inhibitions almost nonexistent.**

***"My book!"***
Both boys and girls of this age group tend to be very fond of *their own* books. They enjoy books with pic-

tures and a few words on the page, with much repetition of both words and ideas. The size and shape of the book may also be important to the twenty-four month old. They tend to enjoy little books, or books with an interesting shape. Age two loves to be read to, and this is an age when parents can get away with skipping certain words or ideas. (At two and a half, however, you'll have to read every word, and *many* times over!)

Favorite topics for stories are the things that he himself does in the day—brushing teeth, taking a bath, dressing. Especially exciting seem to be stories about his favorite possessions, such as his shoes. He may wish to talk to or about the animals or people in the book. He enjoys singing songs, but don't expect him to replicate a tune (if he can, get him into music early!).

### *Role-play*

Two year olds, both boys and girls, enjoy "playing house" with dolls or stuffed animals, and may play with other two year olds briefly. Most of the play in the "house" involves putting the doll or stuffed animal to bed for sleeping. The toddler will painstakingly cover up the doll with covers, perhaps instructing it to "go to sleep, baby." You may also see the toddler play with the doll being sick, asleep, too hot, or too cold.

The doll may be read to, changed, given medicines, taken for a ride, or fed. Sometimes "playing house" doesn't involve dolls at all, but instead involves the child covering himself with any handy piece of material and putting himself to sleep. Role-playing is crucial if two (or more) two year olds play together. The one who suggests the game is always the authority figure, either Mother or Father. The other players will be assigned roles by the authority figure. This may be successful for a time. However, the play usually breaks down in a few minutes and unless it is revived with fresh interest and enthusiasm by an adult it will be abandoned in short order. The twenty-four to thirty month old is making his first attempts at "cooperation"—there will be many lessons to learn along the way!

## Role-playing is crucial if two year olds play together.

The twenty-four month old prefers to stay with adults in many situations because adults can sustain an interest in the objects of play and the roles being played. If the adult is willing to pretend, the twenty-four month old will elaborate several details of the play. The "food" that you are fed at a "tea party" (and both genders play at this) may become cookies, or ice cream, or soup. The "tea" that you have may be grape-flavored, or quickly become apple juice or coffee. Whereas adults are willing to have second, third, or even fourth helpings of "food" at the tea party, other two year can't sustain an interest long enough to keep the game going. But one adult, with a group of two year olds, *can* keep the game going for several minutes.

### In their own world
Socially, the two year old is still fairly focused on *himself* and his daily activities. He may talk to his shoes, or pretend again and again to feed himself, take a bath,

brush his hair, get a haircut, and brush his teeth. His interest is most keen where *he* is the center of attention, and most of his observations about the world come from a first-person point of reference. When he sees someone else fall, he may say, "I didn't fall down"; when someone else is eating, he may say, "My cookie all gone." It's all about his own life experience.

At the same time, the twenty-four to thirty month old is very taken with the notion of imitation, especially of adults in his world. He will still enjoy and seek out the opportunity to make cookies with cookie cutters, help put biscuits into the oven to bake, sweep the kitchen floor, dust the furniture. The wise parent will seek chances to help the child be involved in an activity, to make what the parent perceives to be "work" into what the two year old perceives to be a "game." This is sometimes hard for parents to do if they are in a hurry to get things done quickly. But remember that wherever you can, involving the twenty-four to thirty month old will be rewarded with smiles, trust, and a sense of confidence on the part of the child.

> **The wise parent will seek chances to help the child be involved in an activity.**

How patient God is with each of us! Just imagine having the capacity to speak (or sing) whole galaxies into existence, and then being willing to wait for thickheaded, thick-hearted human beings to recognize and follow the truth. By comparison, the effort spent waiting for our toddlers to learn from their mistakes as they "help us" seems minimal. How incredible the love that surrounds and sustains each of us.

### *Imitating God*

And how often are we willing to imitate God in our "play" or "work." (I'm certain those two activities are more the same to God than we realize.) Do we scramble to God's elbow, as it were, in eager anticipation of being near divine love, just as our toddler eagerly climbs up on the kitchen chair as we make dinner? As you watch your child imitate your every action and as you see him light up when you invite him into your world, recall that the God of all creation wants us to enter Love's world also—and God hopes, with perfect hope and perfect patience, that you will choose to imitate love in all that you do.

## Language Skills: The Wonderful World of Sentences

Your toddler is now well beyond the stage of producing "jargon," and you will find that he has much to say. Most twenty-four to thirty month olds will be able to converse in three-word sentences, and so can get across to the listener somewhat sophisticated ideas. The toddler's vocabulary may be 200–300 words at this point, and he tends to speak in three-word sentences or phrases that contain nouns, prepositions, and possibly verbs. You may find that when he learns a new word, he uses it to convey a variety of meanings or to cover a broad range of experiences. For example, "mommy" may be used for the child's own mother or for any adult female, although there is usually *some* verbalization that indicates his own mother from others. "Hurt" or "ouch" may be used in every sentence for a few days or weeks, until he seems to have the concept down.

The twenty-four to thirty month old expresses ideas about himself as "me" or by using his own first name, but "I" is usually not part of his repertoire. His own name is particularly fascinating to the two year old, and you will see him actively strengthening the link between *himself* and his name. Two year olds can be quite upset if they are called by a name other than their own, although sometimes this can be a source of great humor to them, especially if an adult makes "guessing your name" into a game. He may or may not clearly distinguish animate from inanimate objects in the world, and so may talk with trees, cars, and toys, and may attempt to ride the bicycle he sees in a book. This is the age when the bedtime ritual of saying "goodnight" to all the objects in the room may become important (if you don't have a copy of the book *Goodnight Moon,* this is the time to get one!).

### A new voice

Your child at this age loves to use his voice for sound effects, also. He may go "swoosh" as he runs the car over the carpet, or "zoom zoom" as the train goes rolling along the kitchen floor. You may also see him give himself directions as he runs through the house. He may in fact talk to himself every bit as much as he talks to other people. Talking, at this age, is still a running accompaniment to activity, but it is also used to convey information and ideas. The twenty-four to thirty month old may begin to describe objects using adjectives— *big, good, little,* and *fast* seem to be among the first descriptors.

> **The twenty-four to thirty month old loves to use his voice for sound effects.**

## Putting words together

Word combinations, such as "no shoes," have become sentences by this age. This process is so gradual that parents are often unaware of how much effort the child is putting forth in the process of developing "fluid" speech. Gradually, the number of words increases in the sentence from three to four to five to six, and one by one, articles, prepositions, and other words enter the sentences. Grammar is not important and not correct at this stage, although meaning may be conveyed with the limited grammar available to the child. ("Us go visit him" is an example of a sentence in which the grammar is incorrect, but the meaning is unmistakable.)

Your child may also be learning the word yes (what a blessing after months of no!), and may begin to form *questions* with words. Why? is sometimes learned—if not used appropriately yet—and may be the child's first answer to questions posed to him. (Later you will hear why questions by the hundreds.) He may also begin to consider *who* issues: the ball was thrown, but who threw it? We heard a bark, but who barked? The wise parents of the twenty-four to thirty month old will expose their child to size, shape, texture, and color statements in abundance, as the child explores the world. He learns "rough" by feeling a rough surface and having the word repeated; he learns "big" by seeing it portrayed in pictures and in real life objects.

Parents who read to their children can initiate conversations about the things and people seen in the stories they read: "Show me the *big* giant"; "Where is the *red* dog?" are questions that the twenty-four to thirty month old loves to answer. It is the beginning of conversation with the parent.

### Actions speak louder

Although word development is a significant aspect of this age, it's important to note that early two year olds may respond better to a bit of rough-housing play than they do to a flurry of words. The child's body, with which he has been working for the past one and a half years, is somehow more familiar to him, and therefore less vulnerable, than his mind or personality. He may react more to physical action than he does to words addressed to him because the physical activity seems less threatening. Since fathers are often the ones who approach the child with more physically-oriented child play, the child—knowing he is about to be tickled, flung (a short distance) into the air, or swung around as if "flying"—may be quite happy to see Daddy. Mothers should be aware of this and not take it personally!

### Childlike prayers

Isn't what we learn about prayer much like the

language-skill development of the twenty-four to thirty month old? Our earliest efforts at communicating with God may be about objects in the world or experiences we have had in the course of our day. Later, we may add ideas and thoughts, feelings and nuances to our communication with the Almighty. Just as the toddler does, we *have* those thoughts and feelings well before we think to tell them to God. It is only over time, and with much practice, that we can learn to articulate the thoughts and feelings we already have into a form of prayer.

> **When you watch your toddler mutter to himself all day long, remember that he is teaching you about the constancy of prayer.**

I think one of the most delightful observations of the child this age is the fact that he talks to himself, giving himself directions even as he moves at a whirlwind pace through his days. When I see a two year old involved in deep conversation with himself, I am reminded that we are to make prayer part of our daily activities in addition to being part of a quiet, meditative time of the day. The twenty-four to thirty month old literally comments to himself on each element of his day. "Jump now" he says, then jumps. "Go dis way" he says, and then runs down the hall. How wonderfully transparent he is, how clear about his actions and intent. When you watch your toddler mutter to himself all day long, remember that he can teach you about the constancy of prayer. If ever anyone could be a model for the idea "pray without ceasing," it is the two-year-old toddler.

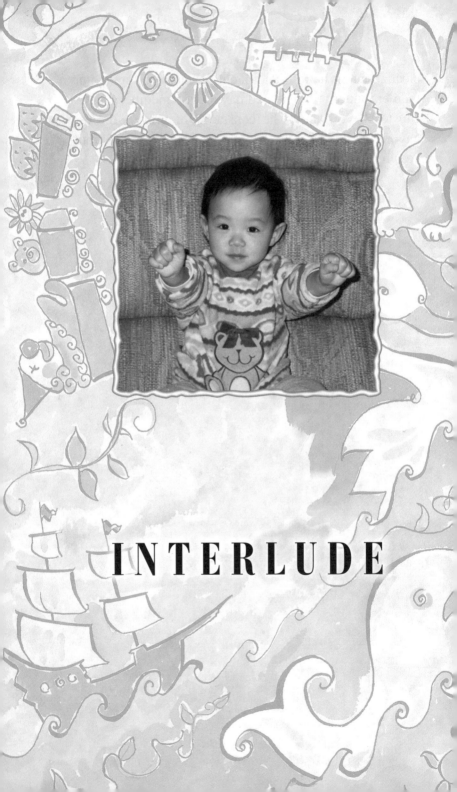

# INTERLUDE

# More about Talking and Prayer

*The most beautiful thing we can experience*
*is the mysterious.*
—Albert Einstein, physicist/mathematician

The two year old (twenty-four to thirty months, especially) is most likely to talk with himself, next most likely to talk with an adult, and least likely to talk with other children his own age. Most of his talk is self-initiated rather than in response to something that was said to him. There is probably a better than even chance that he won't respond even if you talk to him—in most settings, he demands to be the one who initiates conversation. Typically, he is the one who will initiate ·with, "Look, Daddy, dog!" and then expect Daddy to comment. He may then turn to other adults and share with them, "I show Daddy dog."

As he expresses his running commentary about the world in two- or three-word sentences, the two year old makes simple statements about his environment, his family, and the things he does and does not wish to do. He may request help with words, or by clinging to an adult hand and moving the adult to the need (for example, dragging the adult to the refrigerator in order for the child to get a drink of juice). He may explain his own imaginary play and he may begin to ask simple questions. What little conversation he has with another child is often a warning to "keep off" his toys, or a claim "that's mine."

The child this age still *refuses* a request by using motor skills, however. He may stamp his foot, fall to the floor in a tantrum, or just walk away from the adult making the request. Only later will his verbal skills be good enough to make his refusal with words, or (much later) to set up a negotiation with the adult at hand. For now, if requested to give a toy to another child, he may relinquish it to the parent and then run around in circles for a moment. If requested to sit at the dinner table, he may get off the chair and exit the room.

### Staying to talk

How like two year olds we can be sometimes. When someone asks us to do something for the kingdom of God, is our natural reaction to *talk* about it with God in prayer and with our fellow Christians in conversation, to discuss our hesitations and be vulnerable about our doubts? Or do we merely "exit the room" altogether? Maturity often means staying to converse. It's hard. It takes work and practice. It means developing a vocabulary that communicates what we want to say, and it's personally threatening sometimes. But in the long run, it's the only way to have meaningful conversation with God and with other Christians.

In the beginning of our spiritual journey, we may talk to God about our relationship with God more than we talk to other believers. We notice the evidence of God's mercy and grace around us and are thankful for those signs. It is often only later that we begin to share the deep issues of our faith with another human being. We have much to learn about how to express our thoughts, our feelings, our hesitations, and our doubts to someone else, just as a toddler has much to learn about real communication.

God loves us *with* our imperfections, not *in spite of* them. How well do we love God's people *with* their imperfections, instead of *in spite of* them? If we, as adults, could remember how to be unself-conscious in our faith-talk, how to be unassuming and *real* with our God in prayer and with our fellow Christians on the journey, the world—and the church—would be a different place.

# Chapter 6
# Practice Makes Perfect:
## Thirty to Thirty-Six Months

Your thirty month old is now becoming her own person, at least in her own mind! She can move around easily and express more complete thoughts to those around her, but her awareness is still focused on herself as the primary player in the universe. She is sweet sometimes, shy sometimes, charming sometimes, and willing to be the center of everyone's attention all of the time. But whatever she is, it is because *she* chooses it.

Experts in pediatric developmental medicine will tell you that two years is a relatively calm, easy stage of life—it's really two and a half (thirty months) that gives parents fits. This is because the child has, overnight, matured into a stage of what child-development experts Ames and Ilg call *disequilibrium*. This is a time when the child appears to be testing the limits every moment.

In addition, the thirty month old seems highly critical of the parents, and quite petulant in her unwillingness to cooperate with parents, to "go with the program" (as many of the Microsoft-employee parents that come to my practice say).

# Understanding Individual Development

Before we begin our exploration of the thirty to thirty-six month old, I must say a brief word of caution: *your* thirty month old may be a breeze compared to many. Some thirty month olds never exhibit the "terrible twos" behavior—they save it up until age four! Others will not land on the rocky two stage until very late two or even early three. And a few precocious types will begin the two-and-a-half developmental work at twenty-six or twenty-eight months. If your child does not fit the timing of this stage down to the month, don't be alarmed. She will go through some of it, if only briefly. All children have their own timing for developmental progress, and no two children are going to be exactly alike.

> **All children have their own timing for developmental progress.**

So if you see your child begin the time of disequilibrium at two and a half years, thank God that she is "right on schedule." If she is early, be grateful that you will get through it sooner than you would have. (Remember, approximately six months of relative calm "equilibrium" when the child is easy, flexible, and cooperative will follow the six months of disequilibrium!). If she is later in her quest for limits, breathe easy while the calm is with you, and know that God will see you through this stage of parenting every step of the way. Whenever your toddler begins to exhibit the testing-all-limits phase of life is "normal" for your particular child. Comparing your child's developmental timing to every other child you know of the same chronological age will only lead to frustration and anxiety.

Why do developmental stages vary so much in chronological time at this stage of life? It has to do with many factors—age is only one. We also have to take into consideration not only the child's age but her gender, birth order (is she the first-born? the middle child? the end-of-the-line?), learning style (is she a large motor skills person or a small motor/language person?), genetic "programming," and general cognitive motivation for exploring the world around her. No two children are alike in all of these areas. Even identical twins have a "first-born" and a "second-born," and they tend to differentiate themselves along the lines of those birth-order roles from the moment they are born. (I have one set of triplets in my practice who are very *definitely* first-, second-, and third-born children in the family unit.) The reader will understand the difficulties in writing any book that attempts to address "development" in human children, when human children are so varied in their behavior!

Keeping in mind that your toddler may begin to show you thirty-month stormy behavior at twenty-six months, or thirty months, or thirty-five months of age, let's look at some of the characteristics of this age in a toddler's life.

# Large Motor Skills: Coordination R Us!

The thirty month old is beginning to emerge as a fairly coordinated creature. Now she can walk on tiptoe (which she may do frequently) and can do a fine jump with both feet—the standing broad jump improves daily. She may be able to stand on one foot and will do this for anyone who requests it. She can slide down the playground slide, and climb quite successfully.

She also has the ability to regulate some of these actions—as in speeding up, slowing down, dodging obstacles, turning corners, making a sudden stop and then commencing motion once again. She can step *over* an obstacle (which, when you think about it, is a rather sophisticated thing to do). Sometime before age three she will probably be able to throw, kick, and catch a ball, using the arms and the whole body to make the catch.

### Learning right and left
The child may have the first sense of left versus right as she manipulates objects throughout the day. Note here that most children have not made the assignment of left-handed or right-handed yet, and you will see your toddler use either hand with equal ease. She may be eating with the spoon in her right hand because that was the side of the plate on which she found the spoon. But she may just as easily transfer the spoon to the left hand if she decides to grab something else with the right. Most children will not have a designated hand to their motor

skills until three or even three and a half years (forty-two months) of age. (When she reaches the age of cutting out designs in construction paper, note with which hand the scissors get used. That's probably your best clue as to "handedness.")

> **Most children will not have a designated hand awareness until three or even three and a half years of age.**

By left versus right awareness, I mean that the toddler begins to understand that with the second hand she might repeat the action done by the first hand, or with the second foot replicate a movement she tried with the first foot. She begins to think in terms of Experiment #1 as try-some-new-movement-with-the-left-hand, and then immediately Experiment #2 must follow: try-that-same-movement-with-the-right-hand. She will very quickly begin to see that the two hands are *mirror images* of each other: whereas the thumb is on the left side when you look at your *right* hand, the thumb is on the right when you look at your *left* hand (this is with the palm facing away from you). This allows for the replication of movements between the two hands, but it also allows for the child to begin to use the two hands *together* in some new and interesting ways.

The previously mentioned hand game of "here is the church and here is the steeple" is one way to use the hands together. In that game, the two thumbs are side-by-side. When it comes to catching a ball, it's very helpful to have the two thumbs together as the hands close around the ball. For lifting a heavy object, two hands together, with eight fingers curled around the object, is best. And certainly when it's time to put on a jacket or a sweater or a shirt, it's helpful to have the *left* arm go into the *left arm* hole. So the toddler this age is working with the concept of "left and right" in every facet of life.

### *Repeat after me*

A skill related to the above awareness of left and right is the refining of repetitive motions. At this age the child doesn't just jump once, but jumps and literally bounces on her feet *dozens* of times in a row. Now the child doesn't just clap the hands together once or twice, but may walk around the house clapping the hands by the hour—to music that the parent can hear, or perhaps to the beat of a "different drummer," as Emerson says. Now she gets on the tricycle and pedals around and around and around and around . . . the same movement of legs and feet the three millionth time as it was the first time. These repetitive movements are something she delights in, especially when they also accomplish the larger purpose of *moving* her from point A to point B.

Coordination of eyes with hands can be practiced with repetitive movement as can coordination of hearing with spatial relationships (for example, the child who walks around nodding her head no is experimenting with the way sounds change when we move our head in a quick, repetitive fashion). And the toddler is now differentiating repetitive sensory nervous system signals into the awareness in time and space of the hands and the feet in unique ways.

### The eyes have it

The central nervous system (CNS) at this toddler stage is figuring out that we use our eyes to give cues to our *hands* in very different ways than we give cues to our *feet*. That is, when we wish to accomplish a motor movement with the hands, repetitive or not, we usually *look* at the hands as we work. When we wish to accomplish a motor movement with our legs and feet, we may look at them the first few times as we "learn" the motion and then very quickly count on our legs and feet to find their own proprioceptive sense without the aid of our visual sense.

The toddler this age is learning this skill with the use of the tricycle or pedal car. She may study her legs with the first few go-rounds, and then as she learns the motion, she doesn't look at her legs and feet anymore. This ability to do repetitive movements involving motion of either hands or feet without looking at them is called *diadokokinesis,* and the inability to do them in a coordinated fashion is called *dysdiadokokinesis.* (No wonder it seems that doctors are speaking a foreign language sometimes!) Visually challenged children will learn the same diadokokinetic motions, but it will take them a bit longer to count on the reliability of those movements.

### Practice, practice

There is a lesson here for the student of spirituality as well as the student of toddler behavior: What we practice, we get better at. The toddler studies how to make the legs and feet propel the tricycle so that she needn't look at the feet as she flies around the driveway or down the sidewalk. By practicing the repetitive movement, she gives herself the opportunity to move down the sidewalk (using legs and feet) while looking at other things in the environment. She is creating for herself the chance to learn more about the world, and it all comes from the practice inherent in repetitive movements.

God is so wise! We were created with the ability to learn from repetition and we can use that to our advantage. By practicing prayer, meditation, reading of Scripture, and worship, we actually progress and grow in our faith over time. When we have these spiritual disciplines at work in our lives, we are free to "go new places" in our relationship with God. We are freeing ourselves up to see new insights into the nature of God's love and mercy, to envision new and creative avenues of ministry, to follow our Shepherd to the heights.

> **We were created with the ability to learn from repetition.**

The next time you see your own toddler, or one of the neighborhood children, moving down the sidewalk on a tricycle, remember the gift of repetition as a learning tool. Recall the new places that the spiritual disciplines in your life can take you as you learn more about loving and trusting your Creator, and thank God for the toddler who illustrates it for you along the way.

# Small Motor Skills: Home is the "Imagination Station"

Fine motor skills have also continued to improve in this age group. Your toddler is now able to differentiate her fingers from her hand as a unit, and her hands are not as likely to open and close as a single entity. Her fingers are not as apt to close up as you struggle to get her mittens on, for example. Also, as her hand differentiation develops during the year, she shows you less and less of the earlier simultaneous action of both hands. She is more and more able to use only one hand to do work, especially when that work involves the use of tools.

She can do all of the things she could do six months ago, but now she does them more skillfully. Putting macaroni noodles or beads on a string is easier now, and fewer macaronis are spilled in the process! Painting or making marks on paper with a crayon is still fairly abstract with regard to the product, but the muscles used are more of the lower arm and not so much the "whole arm" approach of the two year old. You may even see the wrist bend with each crayon stroke. She is better with puzzles and even more masterful in manipulating small toys or parts of toys. Remember, handedness—in most cases—is still not determined.

### Creative energy

So your toddler goes through her days with an avid interest in portraying the world around her, through imaginative play (which almost always replicates her life experiences, though she is usually cast in a more authoritative role), and through arts and crafts as well. She may be fascinated with the idea of gluing something onto something else. (Glue sticks are a wonderful invention!) She is able to create "pictures" with the use of paper and crayons or paint, and these pictures tell a lot about her life, her daily routines, her observations about the world.

One thing I counsel parents with toddlers this age is: When presented with one of your child's creations, don't look at it and then say, "What is it?" The child may be upset or offended that you couldn't distinguish the blue slash marks as a house, or the orange circular scribbles as the tree in the front yard. Worse, she may feel as if she has failed in some fashion because you couldn't figure it out without help. A better approach is to admire it for a few seconds and then say, "Tell me about this," or "You must have worked hard on this." Focusing more on the *process* and less on the *product* at this point will give your child the self-esteem boost she needs to say to herself, "I can do this!" You will see countless other creations before this stage is finished, and that is as it should be. Don't be a source of negative feedback about your child's artwork at this stage. Just admire the work it took to produce it and remind her that she is loved.

> **Focusing more on the *process* and less on the *product* at this point will give your child a self-esteem boost.**

## *The God of encouragement*

Consider what God's perspective might be: Here we are, poor humans who struggle so often with inconsequential things and who work furiously in our lives to *produce*. We scribble, we cut and paste, we "create" our lives and often their problems. Then, proud of our accomplishments and waiting for approval, we bring the result to our heavenly Parent. How many thousands of times has God looked at our proud scribbles, scratched the divine head and thought, "What *is* it?" Our spiritual awareness is often much weaker than we realize.

Yet, God never says, "You dummy! When will you get it right?" God looks at our intentions and our efforts and says, "Good job! You must have worked hard on that project. You are learning about how to live the life of love, how to live in constant connection with me. I love you and I am proud of you. All of your life I will love you. Now go out and speak a word for love again. Tell someone about your own process. Share who you are, and I will continue to show you who you were created to be."

God affirms us in the *process* of growth in our lives, counting the *product* of lesser importance. Our Creator encourages us in our successes, gives us strength in our weakness, and sends us back to the drawing table—or the painting easel, or the cutting board, or the committee meeting, or the piano, or the word processor—to try again. The God of encouragement is always with us, always nudging us forward in our lives and in our awareness of creative grace.

As you watch your toddler labor over a "creation," be amazed at her instinctive need to express herself. Remember that the need to express ourselves and share the process of living with one another is a uniquely human characteristic that is a gift from God. Admire your toddler's labor, and know that God admires your labors. Affirm this child whom you love so dearly (even if you can't always get in touch with that feeling of love on a moment's notice!), and recall that God affirms your life, your work, your emotions, your very being. When your toddler brings a creation for your admiration and approval, remember that the God of all creation is thrilled whenever you bring one of your scribbles to the throne of grace, place it on the lap where you've been cradled and cared for, and say, "Look, Daddy! I did it for you!" Keep scribbling.

## Social Skills: Exploration and Story-Telling

The thirty month old is becoming a social creature, but her problem-solving skills are not particularly adaptive yet. Her perception and her comprehension are still immature, and so she has few tools with which to solve a problem situation. For example, if confronted with a door blocked at its base with a stick or doorstop, she will try over and over to close the door just by pushing—it is the rare thirty month old who thinks to look down to discover what might be keeping the door from closing. In trying to fit pieces into a puzzle, she might try pushing or even pounding the pieces *harder* in order to make them fit, rather than turning them to fit the shape required. (This is reminiscent of the traveler who speaks *louder* when trying to make himself understood in a foreign language.)

Many new abilities are seen at thirty months of age that were not present at two years of age. The toddler can now imitate vertical and horizontal strokes and can make a cross on paper. She can build a tower of up to eight cubes. She can repeat two numbers spoken to her. She loves to hear stories and enjoys the rhythm and the rhyme of words. She now wants to hear a story read to her word-for-word, exactly the same each time, with nothing left out. (The sharp thirty month old will catch any omission parents may attempt!)

> **She enjoys stories that focus on her own life and its activities.**

She enjoys stories that focus on her own life and its activities. These stories can be about waking up, getting dressed, taking a bath, playing outside, or going to the store. She may also enjoy stories that give factual information about animals or modes of transportation—and there is no question in the mind of the thirty to thirty-six month old that bears *do* talk, that Frances the Badger can live in a family, or that Frog and Toad can be friends and share adventures. This is a wonderful age at which to begin telling stories of events from the Bible because the children absorb the information so readily and are fascinated with the details of daily living in biblical times. Plot has little place in the story for this age group, but a plot that is repeated can be absorbed over time. Children at this age enjoy role playing, with ever greater accuracy. All of the adult behaviors that the child has seen will be acted out: feeding a stuffed animal, dressing a baby doll, talking on the telephone, driving a car.

### Hands-on activity

Fingerpainting is a good activity for this age group, probably better than painting with a brush. With the advent of color-already-in-the-page painting books, the child has merely to brush water onto the paper in order to make color happen in the picture (some educators, particularly visual arts teachers, rail against these, however). Play-Doh is also a great medium for this age group: the thirty to thirty-six month old will roll coil after coil of "rope" in Play-Doh and then construct other figures with the coils. Mud and sand are also good activities for this age. In the very earliest stages of playing together with other children of similar age, sand is especially good because there is usually *lots* of it (i.e., a sandbox or the beach), and therefore most children don't get stuck in arguments over whose sand it is—there is enough sand for everyone!

The thirty to thirty-six month old enjoys playing with toys that can be taken apart and put back together again, such as Legos, building blocks, cars and trucks that can be disassembled and reconfigured. She shows a distinct preference for toys of *her own,* and may chastise any other child who attempts to play with *"her"* toys. Usually she has dolls or stuffed animals that she will line up and speak to, "discipline," or give advice to. She may also have a security blanket or some other object that must be with her at all times.

## *Go for a walk*

Toddlers this age enjoy short excursions too. They prefer adventures around the neighborhood, close to their everyday environment, more than elaborate ones. It is as if the toddler wishes to venture into the unknown in *very small* steps, changing the view of one house on the street at a time. When you find yourself saying no one hundred times in a row, it may be *very* constructive for you and your child to go for a walk. This reminds the parent that it *is* possible to have a pleasant few minutes with the toddler and reminds the toddler that every word out of the parent's mouth isn't no. All in all, short walks in almost any weather can be very refreshing for the mind and spirit, as well as for the revitalization inherent in changing the visual environment. (I say "any weather" because we Pacific Northwesterners learn to walk in all kinds of weather, most of them wet!)

## *Abundant love*

The toddler does best—when attempting to play with another child—in an environment of unlimited resources, such as the beach where there is unlimited sand. And God is gracious to provide this kind of "unlimited" resource for the toddler. God is also very good about providing adult humans with unlimited resources of *love* for purposes of getting us to "play with others" in a cooperative fashion. When we worry that there may not be enough love, when we get antsy about how much (and in what fashion) we are acknowledged and appreciated for our efforts, we are saying, in essence, that we don't believe there is enough love to go around. But God is *infinite* love and grace and therefore we cannot "use up" God's love, nor can someone else in the kingdom of God use up all of God's love and attention. As Augustine stated, "God loves each of us as if there were only one of us."

### Changing times

The other characteristic of God the thirty- to thirty-six-month-old toddler reminds us of is this: The toddler enjoys very *small* increments of change in her world, her environment. She feels less threatened and more comforted by surroundings that she knows. Human beings resist change in *anything.* Fortunately, the God who created us seems to know this about us and will never push us to change more than we can handle. We may feel that we are being asked to change everything due to a death, a move, a broken relationship. Yet God often allows some things to remain steady in the midst of the turbulence. As we grow in our faith-experience and in our reliance on the Creator of the universe, perhaps we (as adults) will get to the point at which, by clinging to God's hand, we can let go of all the other details of our lives and understand that the only truly unchanging thing in the cosmos is the God whose hand we hold.

> **The God who created us will never push us to change more than we can handle.**

When we arrive at that spiritually mature place, we

realize that all we need is God. The apostle Paul said this when he remarked, "for me to live is Christ." When God's love is our first and only true desire, we are able to pick up our lives from a comfortable town in Switzerland and move to Kenya in order to be a missionary doctor there. When we are so confident that the guiding hand of God is all we need, we can accept an unfamiliar job, or decide to take those evening college classes— we can even raise a toddler! Watch your thirty- to thirty-six-month-old toddler cling to the familiar while resisting change—and remember that God waits for us, always, to cling to God's love as the most familiar thing we know.

## Language Skills: Just *Say* No!

The thirty- to thirty-six-month-old child of either gender will be able to say her full name and may be able to identify several items from pictures in a book. She refers to herself as "me" or "I" as often as she uses her first name. She will still direct most of her verbalizations to an adult rather than to another child in the room, but she talks to herself less than she did six months ago. (She may still give a running commentary on her actions when playing alone, however.)

Her verbal skills are much more versatile than they were six months ago; her vocabulary seems to increase by increments of dozens of new words weekly, and she can now tell someone about her current activity, a past occurrence, or something she intends to do. She may ask for help and demand *not* to be helped all at once (this is one good illustration of how a child's "logic" doesn't match up to an adult's logic). She can tell you about her own skills, as in "I can jump" or "I'm a big girl now—I can ride the big bike."

She can give and command information freely, but always when *she* wishes to have the information or to make it available to someone else. "Where's the puppy?" may be interspersed with "We have dog food at our house"—all of it jumbled more or less together. She also gives very direct commands to adults: "Get out of my way," "Go get me some cookies," or "You drive me," and she feels more comfortable giving commands to adults than to other children. She may complain about the actions of other children, however, *to* the adult: "He hit me," "She took my toy," "He knocked me down."

### *So much to say*

Still, the thirty- to thirty-six-month-old toddler is most interested in what she herself has to say to an adult, rather than having an *equal* exchange of information. The child of this age may not respond to verbal communication from an adult or to requests for a given action. She may choose to ignore the wishes of the adult or to ignore the adult's presence completely. The toddler of this age has several options for refusing to do what an adult requests of her—she may simply ignore the adult, she may walk away, or she may refuse verbally. But the verbal refusals usually outweigh the walking away refusals by a ratio of three to two. Language refusals at this age consist mostly of a forthright and vehement No!

The thirty-six month old is directing an increasing amount of conversation toward children her own age, but she is still more interested in what she has to say than in listening to what someone else has to say. Direct commands are given in an authoritative voice as she attempts to manipulate the actions of others. Name calling and aggressive threats are also a large part of the verbalization. "Billy, get off that!" "I'll hit you if you don't move," and "You are a bad girl!" can be heard in any group of thirty- to thirty-six-month-old folks. A few of the verbally mature thirty-six month olds can make polite comments to potential playmates, but most wait until the fourth year of life for these.

> **The child of this age may not respond to verbal communication or to requests for a given action.**

Occasionally the thirty-six month old can keep up a running commentary on her own actions, and these are the major factor in her self-initiated "conversations" with other children. For the most part, the thirty-six month old doesn't respond to verbalizations from other children; she may say "Hi" at the most. "Mine" may be the comment when another child picks up a toy she wishes to play with, but true give-and-take conversation is still months or years away.

### Listening prayer
At this stage of life the child is still more interested in—obsessed with—what *she* has to say than in listen-

ing to another person speak to her. Isn't that how we often approach God? We are absorbed in what we have to say to God, but often not very concerned with what God has to say to us. Some of us rarely get to the *listening* aspect of prayer at all. But prayer should be a true give-and-take! We must always be about the business of listening to God's voice in our lives and trying to discern God's direction and advice. We must move beyond our own selfish fascination with what *we* have to say and move into a more mature place to stand in which our primary concern is *listening*—to God's love, and to our fellow human beings. As you struggle to remain patient with *listening* to your thirty- to thirty-six-month-old toddler, remember that God listens to each of us patiently—and waits for us to learn to listen to the voice of Love.

# Conclusion: You've Only Just Begun

By now you can see that all of the skill-groups (large motor, small motor, social, and language/communication) merge together at times and that a skill from one group may build up skills in another group. The child becomes more a jumble of skills all mushed together, depending on his genetic programming, his interests, his body type, his birth order, his learning style. But the one- to three-year-old toddler is a wonder in many arenas. Look back to two years ago and marvel at how much he has learned and accomplished in such a short time.

The thirty-six month old is on the threshold of some wonderfully imaginative times, and the wise parent will accompany the child on many of those imaginative journeys into play, work, daily activities, relationships, expression of emotions, and physical skills. Your toddler is now a preschooler, and the adventures behind you are still less than those adventures ahead. You are about to embark on a time of wild flights of fancy, accompanied (and sometimes *led*) by your preschooler—and what wonderfully refreshing times they are!

Into this often-dreary world of routine, stifled feelings, and general lack of creativity bursts your wild and precious three year old, ready to take you on adventures to the moon, observe the behavior of dinosaurs, and fight fires across the face of the globe—all in a single afternoon. While you may not need to be quite as diligent in chasing your older toddler's body around in order to keep him safe, you will need to be every bit as diligent in chasing your preschooler's imagination across the cosmos, in order to enjoy his adventures and to remind him that you are *with* him, comforting and supporting him in all that he does.

What a gift that we have God as a model for that kind of comfort and support in our own lives. Wise parents will continue, throughout their child's life, to see the parallels between what they do for their child, as parents, and what wondrous love and support God gives to each of us as children of God. (If you've survived the toddler years somewhat intact, be reassured that you will get through the early adolescent years, too—in fact, in many ways they will remind you of your toddler's lessons!)

Be patient with yourself in your role as parent—you really *are* doing the best you can. Be patient with your child as he moves through new and murky depths of developmental progress—he really *does* have a good heart, and at any given moment in time he is doing at a fast and furious pace the work of his developmental stage. Know, and remind him verbally, that he *is* a "good kid"—he is in process, just as are all human beings.

In loving the child in this difficult phase the parents mirror the unconditional love of God. Perhaps bringing about this type of love is the child's role at this time of his life—just as you were a toddler who experienced God's love through your parents' lives, and they experienced love from their parents, and so on back to Eden's lush paradise.

Parent boldly, imaginatively, and laughingly, and remember that you cannot out-love God, who gave you this wonderful bundle of energy you call your child. Blessings on your continued journey!

# Further Reading

Ames, Louise Bates and Frances L. Ilg. (Gesell Institute of Human Development). *Your Two Year Old: Terrible or Tender.* New York: Delta, 1976.

Ames, Louise Bates, Frances L. Ilg, and Carol Chase Haber. (Gesell Institute of Human Development). *Your One-Year-Old: The Fun Loving, Fussy 12 to 24 Month Old.* New York: Delta, 1982.

Brazelton, T. Berry. *Toddlers and Parents: A Declaration of Independence.* New York: DTP Publishers, 1989.

Dobson, James C. *Coming Home: Timeless Wisdom for Families.* Wheaton, IL: Tyndale, 1999.

———. *Discipline with Love,* Wheaton, IL: Tyndale, 1983.

———. *Parenting Isn't for Cowards.* Nashville, TN: Word, 1987.

———. *The Strong-Willed Child.* Wheaton, IL: Tyndale, 1978.

Faber, Adele and Elaine Mazlish. *How to Talk So Kids Will Listen and Listen So Kids Will Talk.* New York: Avon, 1991.

Faull, Jan. *Mommy! I Have to Go Potty!: A Parent's Guide to Toilet Training.* New York: Raefield-Roberts, 1996.

Ferber, Richard. *Solving Your Child's Sleep Problems.* New York: Simon & Schuster, 1986.

Fraiberg, Selma H. *The Magic Years: Understanding and Handling the Problems of Early Childhood.* New York: Fireside, 1996.

Holt, Pat and Grace Ketterman. *When You Feel Like Screaming!* Wheaton, IL: Harold Shaw, 1988.

Kurcinka, Mary Sheedy. *Raising Your Spirited Child.* New York: HarperPerennial, 1992.

Miller, Kathy Collard. *When Counting to 10 Isn't Enough.* Wheaton, IL: Harold Shaw, 1996.

Pantley, Elizabeth. *Kid Cooperation.* New York: New Harbinger, 1996.

Parish, Ruth Ann. *Your Baby's First Year: Spiritual Reflections on*

*Infant Development.* Wheaton, IL: Harold Shaw, 1997.

Pinker, Steven. *The Language Instinct.* New York: HarperCollins, 1995.

Shelov, Stephen P. and Robert Hanneman, eds. *Caring for Your Baby and Young Child.* New York: Bantam Doubleday Dell, 1998.

Turecki, Stanley. *The Difficult Child.* New York: Bantam Doubleday Dell, 1989.

Weissbluth, Marc. *Healthy Sleep Habits, Happy Child.* New York: Fawcett, 1987.